HAVING DONE ALL,

Stand

A MOTHER'S JOURNEY THROUGH
A BROKEN ADOPTION

Sheila Conley

ISBN 978-1-64559-309-6 (Paperback)
ISBN 978-1-64559-310-2 (Digital)

Cover design by Bruce Norris

Covenant Books, Inc.
11661 Hwy 707
Murrells Inlet, SC 29576
www.covenantbooks.com

Therefore take up the whole armor of God,
that you may be able to withstand in the evil day,
and having done all, to stand.
                                    —Ephesians 6:13

CHAPTER 1

I can do all things through Christ
who gives me strength.
—Philippians 4:13

I had never heard a four-year-old child scream so loudly before or reach such an ear-piercing pitch without there being lots of blood or a broken bone. His screams of panic were echoing off the tile walls and filling the brightly lit restroom. I hadn't expected him to react in such an extreme way. He took me completely off guard.

I made the mistake of asking him to potty before we boarded the airplane. He barely shook his head no when I asked if he needed to go, but with him being so young, I figured it wouldn't hurt to have him give it a try. After all, it was about nine in the morning, and he had yet to go for the day. We had been up for hours. The last thing I wanted to do was squeeze both of us into an airplane toilet during our flight. I wasn't even sure if that was possible. Going now would just be so much easier on both of us—or so I thought.

I led him into a stall with me. I used the toilet first and then encouraged him to give it a try. When I traded places with him, he panicked and started pushing against me to get to the door. When I opened it, he quickly backed out a few steps and then dropped himself to the floor. It was immediately obvious that he was afraid to turn his back to me. His eyes were wide with panic as he scooted himself up against the far wall.

It really wasn't that serious of a situation, so if he didn't want to go, there was no reason for me to try to force him. If me suggesting he potty causes him to panic and fear me, I can just as easily forget it, and we can simply move on. I tried to communicate that, but when

I spoke directly to him, he started screaming in terror with his little arms and legs swinging wildly in my direction. He clearly wanted me to stay far away from him. I had no idea what triggered him to be so fearful. I definitely needed to find a way to diffuse the situation before it escalated any further.

I stepped over to the sinks and slowly washed my hands. I wanted to give him a moment to calm himself down and to realize that I wasn't going to force him to go. His screaming began to subside, but his eyes remained fixed on me. Out of the corner of my eye, I could see him flinching every time I made the slightest movements even though I was a good distance away and completely out of arm's reach.

As I stepped in his direction toward the paper towel dispenser, his body stiffened, and he pressed himself more firmly to the wall. He was sure I was going to strike him when I ripped off some paper to dry my hands. The noise made him jump, and his little arms flew up in defense of his face. His eyes continued to follow me as I slowly gathered up our winter coats and extended the handle on my carry-on luggage to indicate that we were moving on. When I turned toward him and let him know it was time to head to our gate, he started flailing his arms and kicking his legs again to ensure that I kept my distance while half-crying, half-screaming, "No!"

Any effort I made to calm him seemed to only escalate his panic. With every word I spoke, he just screamed louder. What in the world has happened to this little boy to garner such a reaction of this magnitude? Was he terrified of public toilets? Had I been too pushy? Why was he so scared of me? He seemed perfectly fine just moments before. I had no idea what to do. Nothing seemed to calm him down or assure him I wasn't going to hurt him in any way. I found myself standing there watching him in bewilderment.

I tried exiting the restroom to see if he would follow me, but of course he didn't. His screaming stopped when he saw me disappear around the corner, but I couldn't just leave him there alone. I went back in and tried to encourage him to come with me, but he only pressed himself against the wall with more determination. I think he would have run if there was an alternative exit because his breath was quick and shallow, and his eyes started darting around the room like he was looking for an escape route.

I could see it on his face when he realized that the only way he could get out of the room was to walk right past me. I was standing between him and the doorway. I remained, still hoping his realization wouldn't push him back over the edge. He seemed to be barely holding himself together. After a few minutes of us staring at each other in a tenuous silence, I offered him my hand so that I could help him up. I knew immediately to withdraw by observing his physical response to my outstretched hand. It was evident that any direct engagement from me would be counterproductive.

I glanced around the restroom assessing my options. We couldn't just stay there all day. We have a plane to catch, and time was ticking. It was embarrassing to have become the morning's spectacle. The other women in the restroom were trying their best to hide their stares, but the expressions on their faces said it all. I could only imagine how harshly they were judging me and my parenting ability. I had to fight the urge to explain and defend myself, but they had no way of knowing our unique situation. I'm sure they only saw an incompetent mother with her out-of-control child. What they couldn't know is that I wasn't his mother. Not yet anyway. We were practically strangers.

*****

I was in and out in only twelve hours. I had missed all of my connecting flights the day before because a flight attendant had overslept, and his late arrival delayed takeoff by two hours. That delay had me begging for flights in three different airports across the United States. My travel time had been extended from six hours to almost fourteen. By the time I finally landed, the sky was dark, a cold bitter snow had blown in, and I had missed dinner with the foster family.

His few belongings were packed and ready to go by the door when I arrived. The family had bought him a large Christmas train set, just like the one that was whistling and circling under their Christmas tree. They told me how much he loved the train and how he would sit and watch it every evening before bed. They hoped that by giving him one of his own, it would make his transition to his new home a little easier.

I said my hellos and goodbyes to the foster family and their eight adopted children in less than two hours, and then the case-worker drove us over to the Children's Services building. By this time, it was nearing midnight, and I was told there were a few things we needed to pick up from the office. She led me to a large storage room that was filled with everything you would expect if you went into a child's bedroom and tossed all that they owned into large black trash bags. The room was overflowing from what had to have come from a dozen or more children. Each bag was stuffed with clothes, shoes, school papers, art projects, stuffed animals, and all sorts of toys—each child's life crumpled up and discarded.

She found the two trash bags she was looking for and then handed me four bright-yellow duffel bags. She informed me that I only had fifteen minutes to sort through the trash bags to then fill the duffel bags with whatever items I decided I wanted to keep. The rest would be given away. Wait, what? How was I supposed to decide what to pack so quickly? Fifteen minutes was not enough time to discover what was in each bag, let alone choose what was valuable enough to carry forward into his new life.

I didn't even know what size clothes he wore, and when I asked the caseworker, she had no idea either. I had no choice but to try to visualize how big he was in comparison to a typical four-year-old and proceed as best I could. As I began digging, I found a nice leather sandal, but there was no way of knowing where, or even if, there was a mate to it buried somewhere in the mess. The shoe looked brand-new and about the right size, but how would I know without putting it on his foot? Apparently, there wasn't any time for that. As I continued digging and pulling out everything with potential value, I spotted the mate farther down near the bottom of the bag.

I could feel the caseworker's impatience for me to hurry. I assumed she was eager to get home after such a long day. I too was exhausted. My eyes were burning, and I didn't have the energy to complain. I knew it wouldn't do any good anyway. I figured that my silence was best since what I really wanted to do was tell her off every time she glanced at her watch. Fifteen minutes was not enough time! The more pressure I felt, the more upset I became. I couldn't understand how a child's whole life could be tossed away like this. Apparently, moving children by trash bag was acceptable—or at least common enough to fill a room.

What was important to this little boy whom I barely knew? Did he have a favorite toy in here somewhere that he had been missing? If there had been more time, I would have liked to have seen his reaction to what was in the bags, but he was waiting outside in the warm car with his foster mother. Maybe he could have shed some light on what items I should have chosen, but he would have undoubtedly slowed the whole process down. I'm sure that was the reason for bringing the foster mother along and then having them wait in the car together.

At the end of my fifteen minutes, I had managed to grab a handful of preschool crafts that included developmental milestones like handprints and footprints. I had grabbed every photo of him that I could find even if it was crumpled or ripped. Somehow I managed to stuff all four of the duffel bags, but I couldn't help but wonder if I had missed something important. As soon as the last zipper was closed, I was whisked out the door just as quickly as we had arrived.

We pulled up to a strange motel in the dark. The caseworker led us to a room on the second floor, unlocked the door, and said she would be back for us bright and early in the morning. Before I could say anything, she was gone. As soon as the door shut behind her, the little boy realized he was alone with some strange woman and started whimpering. He had no idea where we were or who I was. I didn't really know where we were either.

This was not the smooth transition I was hoping for. Of course, he's going to be scared. I didn't have any idea of how to comfort him, and I realized immediately that he didn't want me to touch him when he backed away from my outstretched hand. Eventually, I was able to distract him by showing him the ice crystals that had formed on the window and how they were sparkling in the light of the street lamp.

Then I gave him a blue Matchbox car to race in the shadows. We eventually drifted off to sleep well past midnight.

Bright and early as promised, she picked us up, and we headed to a restaurant for breakfast. I was told on the way that we were meeting up with his birth mother to give her a chance to say her final goodbye. His little face lit up when he saw her, and he happily climbed into her lap. She handed me a blanket that she had stitched for him when he was a baby, as well as a bright-orange monkey for him to remember her by. She stroked his hair while he ate his pancakes, and one by one, silent tears slowly rolled down her cheeks.

I struggled to fight back tears of my own as I watched her cry. Each bite of my food went down hard, pushing past the lump that had formed in my throat. The caseworker did her best to fill the heavy silences with conversation as we watched the little boy eat contentedly in his mother's lap, completely unaware of the circumstances of the day.

Everything my husband and I had been working toward was finally coming to pass, but my gain also meant her loss. My heart was breaking for the mother sitting before me and for her little boy who was going to be states away and unable to see her again. In spite of the current situation, I knew she loved him deeply. It saddened me to think that with the passing of time, her face was going to fade from his memory.

Once we finished our breakfast, we said our goodbyes, and I assured her he would be well cared for. I promised her that she could contact me anytime and that I would send pictures whenever she asked. She thanked me and hugged him tightly one last time. As we drove away on that cold, snowy morning, I watched her out the rear window. She was standing inside the restaurant watching through the frosty windowpane. I choked back tears all the way to the airport.

*****

I glanced at my watch, and boarding was about to begin. I was determined not to miss all of my connecting flights as I had the day before. He was making no effort to move, and we were running out of time. I balanced his Christmas train box on top of my suitcase, draped our heavy winter coats over my arm, and grabbed his wrist. We were getting out of that restroom, and we were going to get to our gate!

I figured he was going to scream either way, so I decided to just go for it and pull him to his feet. I was able to walk and half drag him out into the corridor before he was successful at clawing and kicking himself free. Now he was yelling "nos," "go aways," and all sorts of curse words at me. I looked around to see if there was anyone that could assist me, but the corridor was practically empty. I assumed someone would alert airport security so that they could question me because it sounded like I was abusing the child with the way he was acting.

I scooped him up off the floor to carry him. That is when he started punching me in the head, kicking his legs, and using all of his might to wiggle free. After only a few steps, I couldn't hold on to him anymore. I had to drop him back down to the floor, letting our luggage and coats topple every which way. At the rate we were going, there was no way the train set was going to make it home in one piece. I might not either for that matter. I debated about just leaving the train set behind, but it was such a thoughtful gift, especially for a little boy whose whole life had been condensed down to only four yellow duffel bags.

I decided to put my heavy fur-lined coat on to free up my hands so that I could try again, but all that did was weigh me down and make me feel like I was going to die of heatstroke. Sweat had starting rolling down my back. I tried to carry him again and again, and each time ended the same way. He was undoing much of the progress we were making by scooting away from me at every chance. It was three steps forward and two steps back.

I even tried to walk away, hoping he would follow me on his own, but he never did. Of course, he wouldn't. He didn't know me, didn't know where we were, and now he was absolutely terrified of me because I was touching him. I'm sure we looked absolutely ridiculous! This was not the sweet homecoming I had envisioned. This was turning more into an abduction rather than an adoption.

Exhaustion was starting to set in. Tears of frustration were sting-ing my eyes, and my head was throbbing from him pounding me with his little fists. My hands and wrists were burning from the fresh scratches, and I just knew I would be covered in bruises the next day. I remember thinking, *How am I going to do this through the next three airports?* I was fighting off the feeling of despair. If only they had let my husband come with me. If he were here, he would be strong enough to carry him and keep his body under control. This was proving to be too much for me to handle on my own, especially with the large train set, our winter coats, and my carry-on suitcase in tow.

I desperately wanted to just give up and walk away. I contem-plated leaving him in the corridor to scream it out all by himself and simply remove myself from the equation. If I'm not there, he has nothing to fear or attack, but you can't just leave a four-year-old alone in the middle of an airport. Then I thought about leaving the luggage behind long enough to get him to the gate, but then I would be in the same situation on the back end. I couldn't leave him alone at the gate while I went back to retrieve our things. I would have no way of knowing how he would behave toward the other passengers, or if he would stay put or run off while I was gone. You're also not supposed to leave your bags unattended. I felt stuck with no viable solution.

I tried to get someone's attention to help me, but the few people around wouldn't stop. They were avoiding eye contact and purposely looking away. An empty airport taxi came speeding down the corri-dor heading in the same direction as our gate. I had a brief moment of hope, thinking someone had called on my behalf, but the driver whizzed by without even a pause. If I would have taken a step to my left, I'm convinced that they would have run me over; they were going so quickly. I would have given everything I had for a ride. If they would have just taken my luggage. I felt completely alone and exhausted. What in the world had I gotten myself into?

*****

I'm not sure how long it actually took us to reach the gate. It was a wrestling match the whole way. I ended up resorting to dragging him by one of his ankles. It didn't stop him from kicking me with the other foot, but it did keep him from punching, clawing, and biting me. It also put him flat on his back and allowed me to drag him with less resistance. I just couldn't believe it had come down to me dragging him. How humiliating. *Hi, I'm your new mom, let me drag you home while you scream in terror.* And whatever happened to offering to help someone in need? Maybe everyone else was too terrified to go near him.

When we finally reached the gate, I let go of his leg, and we both collapsed onto the floor. Instantly he fell silent and curled himself up into a ball as if he knew the battle was over. There was an audible groan when the other passengers realized we would be joining them on their flight. I couldn't blame them. They just watched me wrestle him all the way down the corridor. As I caught my breath, I wondered if our battle would resume when it was time to move again. I desperately prayed it wouldn't. I was so spent that I would have sobbed right then and there if I didn't have an audience.

After a few minutes of silence, everyone's attentions moved on, and I was able to calm down, and reset. What now? I looked over and saw this little boy curled up with his face buried in the floor. The whole day had to be scary for him. His life happened to him and around him in such a way that he wasn't really a part of it, and that had to have created so much insecurity and fear inside of him.

How can a developmentally delayed four-year-old comprehend what it means to move to another state and gain a new mom and dad, especially since he has never had parents in the traditional sense? I just showed up the night before, and everything had happened so quickly. The whole situation had set us up to fail, and it wasn't fair to either one of us.

As people starting boarding, he still wasn't moving. I couldn't tell if he had fallen asleep out of pure exhaustion or if he was just hiding from the world. Suddenly I had an idea. I remembered that I had come prepared. My winter coat had very deep pockets, and in anticipation of the long day of travel ahead of us, I had stuffed crayons, coloring pages, Matchbox cars and trucks, and a variety of superheroes in them.

I checked to see if they were still there, and one by one I pulled out some toys and slid them over in his direction. He didn't raise his head or make a sound, but one little hand slowly reached out and grabbed a superhero and pulled it under himself. Ever so slowly, he uncurled just enough to see what new treasure he had been given. Maybe I should have thought to start with the toys!

Once we found our seats on the plane and buckled our seat belts, I called my husband. At the sound of his voice, I completely broke down into my ugly cry. It takes a lot to push me over the edge, but when that happens, it's just not a pretty sight. My face gets blotchy, my eyes turn bright red, and my nose leaks like a faucet. The first thing that came out of my mouth was how I just couldn't do it and how we had made a horrible mistake.

I shared with him all that had happened as quickly and as quietly as I could manage, but I was struggling not to panic at the thought of fighting him again all alone. I knew I didn't have any more emotional or physical strength left in me. Even though the caseworker had forbidden him to come, my husband apologized for not being there and assured me that I *was* strong enough. It helped to know that he believed in me, but in that moment, I knew I had reached my limit. He had no idea the battle I just went through. Words could never fully describe it.

After everything we had fought for leading up to this day, I had no choice but to see the journey through. When I ended the call, I took a deep breath and pulled out some tissues. I looked up and realized that some of the other passengers were staring at me, and the flight attendants were cautiously watching me from a distance. Maybe I wasn't as quiet as I had hoped. I did my best to gain my composure so I didn't draw any more attention to myself than I already had, but I knew my face was blotchy and my eyes would be bloodshot for a while. I would have welcomed conversation if someone had just asked if I was okay instead of whispering and staring at me.

By the time the airplane took off, the little boy's countenance had changed, and he seemed like a completely different child. He was quiet and expressionless, but I could see a spark of excitement in his eyes as he watched the clouds pass by his window. I settled in and began rehashing the events of my arrival and the foster family I had met. I thought about the things his birth mother had said to me and the bags of belongings I had left behind.

I pulled up my sleeves to check on my bruises and scratches and felt for any lumps on my head. I thought about whether or not I could have done anything differently and formulated a battle plan just in case it happens again when we land. Then I thought of my husband and our three little children who would be waiting for us at the gate. Everything was about to change.

Even with eight hours of travel, he never used the toilet. Not once. Not at the motel that morning, not at the restaurant after breakfast, not during any of the airport layovers. I asked him a few times during the day if he needed to go, and each time he shook his head no. I knew better than to upset our tenuous peace by encouraging him to go when he didn't want to. Apparently, he has an elephant-sized bladder and a will of steel.

Thankfully, we made it home that evening without another incident, and of course, his Christmas train never worked. I almost ditched it a few times along the way, but at least I could say I tried my best to get it home in working order. He didn't seem to notice or express any feelings about that one way or the other. I'm not sure he even realized that the train set was a gift intended just for him.

CHAPTER 2

Trust in the Lord with all your heart
And do not lean on your own understanding.
—Proverbs 3:5

Our lives intersected when he was only eighteen months old, too young for him to remember. The first time I saw him was in the arms of my half brother late one summer evening. Our father had planned a houseboating vacation on his favorite lake, and my brother drove across the Midwest to join us. No one in the family had seen him for many years, and he beamed with pride as he introduced his son, Thomas, to us for the first time.

We noticed rather quickly that Thomas was not like his cousins. He was withdrawn and very quiet. He didn't speak or interact much with the world around him, which was in stark contrast to his cousins, who were running around and loudly exploring every inch of the houseboat. Instead, Thomas sat on the floor at his father's feet, wearing only a diaper with a bottle of milk in his hand.

He was tired and dirty after their long drive, but when I offered to put him to bed for the night, my brother assured me that he would be just fine where he was. When Thomas began to fuss from exhaustion, my brother was quick to tell him to shut up, so he sat on the floor in silence, staring off in the distance until his head slumped forward. He had finally fallen asleep sitting up. His father was busy talking and didn't seem to notice.

Thomas's only nourishment seemed to be his bottle of milk. I didn't see my brother feed him anything else other than a small bite of chocolate. I made it my mission that week to make sure he ate along with the other children, but he didn't seem to know what to do with food. I don't think he liked the way certain foods felt in his mouth, and I'm not sure if he actually swallowed any of it. Most of it, if not all of it, he ended up playing with and then throwing all over the floor. I wasn't sure if he even knew how to consume food that was solid enough to require chewing.

He was mostly nonverbal. He would point, grunt, or yell to us to get our attention. He rarely smiled, but he loved the water. Put him in an inner tube and place him in the water, and he came alive! He would splash and kick with the biggest grin I'd ever seen. When he wasn't in the water, he would just stand on the deck and stare at it. Everyone made sure he spent the whole week in a life vest because none of us knew when he would start to climb overboard. He had no fear or reservation when it came to water, but he seemed to be afraid of just about everything else. It took me five days, but my biggest accomplishment that week was teaching him to say the word *boat*. As far as I know, that was his first real word.

*****

About six months later, our phone rang. We weren't expecting to hear from Children's Services, but my husband, Christopher, and I weren't necessarily surprised. My half brother had spent most of his adult life angry, struggling to hold a job, homeless, drug- and alcohol-addicted, and in trouble with the law. He had been in a long-term on-and-off-again relationship with Thomas's birth mother that seemed very deep and very dysfunctional.

Thomas's birth mother had a tragic childhood that landed her in foster care as a teenager. She had spent those years being sexually abused and had her first child very young. Thomas is her fifth child. She had already lost custody of her other four children: one to their father and the other three to the foster care system. By this time, those three had been adopted out to other families. When I met her, she was struggling with a mood disorder and depression. She admitted to having a long history of alcohol addiction.

According to reports, the police were called to a Kentucky Fried Chicken restaurant one evening where Thomas's birth mother was drunk and causing a scene. When the police car pulled into the parking lot, the officer's report states that he almost hit Thomas, who was wandering outside alone in only a diaper. He was twenty-one months old. She was arrested that evening, and he was immediately placed into foster care.

After a few months of parenting classes, anger management classes, and supervised visits for both biological parents, Children's Services started exploring other placement options for Thomas. They had little hope of him being reunited with either of his birth parents. My brother gave Children's Services our father's name as well as my own as possible caregivers.

The caseworker filled us in on Thomas's current situation and asked us if we would be interested in taking him. She asked me to take some time to consider her request before responding and then to let her know our answer when she called again. I told her we would consider it, but my immediate gut response was absolutely not.

Christopher and I had never discussed adopting. We already had three children who were only three, five, and seven years old. When you add in work and full-time ministry, our days were quite full. We had previously decided that our family of five was complete. I just wasn't sure we could take on more responsibility and everything else that would come along with adoption, but none of those reasons were really the cause of my resistance.

My half brother was in and out of my life growing up. He was very different than my other brother and me. He grew up in a rough inner city area not too far from us. He lived with an alcoholic mother whom I rarely saw, but when I did, she was usually so drunk that she could barely stay on her feet. I always assumed he wasn't cared for very well because he had a lot of problems in school, issues with authority, and run-ins with the law, which had gotten him arrested a few times. I remember visiting him in a group home when he was a teenager.

There was a lot of hurt and anger that my brother held against my father. He lived with him and my mother until he was about nine years old, but then my mother died of breast cancer. My father, being a widower with three young children, sent his eldest son back to live with his mother while he pieced his life back together. As the years went by, my brother openly expressed his anger and jealously toward us. We lived in the suburbs. He was envious of the material things that we owned. I'm sure much of the way he felt was stemmed from his perceived rejection from when he was sent back to live with his mother. I assume it was also compounded by his mother's chronic substance abuse and inevitable neglect.

My father remarried, and my stepmother didn't seem to like him very much; he didn't seem to like her either. There always seemed to be tension in the house whenever he would come for a visit, but I was too young to be aware of the dynamics and reasons behind it all. What I do know is that if there was something we had that my brother wanted, he felt entitled to take as he pleased even if it meant breaking into the house to do so. He stole a lot of our father's tools and his expensive fishing equipment. Inevitably, items around the house would turn up missing after he left.

One summer he was staying with us, and he had brought along a collection of pornographic magazines that he kept hidden under the bed. He cornered me a few times to make me look at them with him while he made very lewd comments. He would come into my bedroom and try to watch me undress. I would hide in my small closet to change, but the closet door was louvered, and he would stand on the other side and try his best to look in at me. Propositioning me to do sexual things to him wasn't out of the ordinary, so naturally he made me extremely uncomfortable. I did everything I could to avoid him and not be caught alone with him. I was thankful that as I got older, his visits became shorter and less frequent.

I was not interested in intricately involving myself in my brother's life now that we were adults. I have always found his behavior unpredictable. You never knew when he would get angry. One minute we would be having a nice conversation, and then he would flip out about how much I and my other brother were judging him or how much better we thought we were than him. I believe he suffers from mental illness. If my husband and I were going to raise his son, one of my immediate concerns was on how much he would become involved in our lives. There was a high probability that he would cause us problems.

I also understood generational iniquity enough to be concerned that we would be raising a child that would end up acting a lot like his biological father. I wasn't interested in making a lifelong commitment to raising his son and potentially have to deal with a repeat of all the same issues I witnessed growing up. Only this time, it would be full-time, every day, and I would be the parent dealing with it all.

Even though I wanted to say no right away, Christopher and I decided to pray about it and then talk more the next morning. Honestly, I didn't really pray. It was more like pleading than praying. I spent that night begging God not to ask me to do it, but every time I got quite for a minute, I already knew that I needed to. After all, how could I abandon my nephew to the foster care system? What would happen to him if I really said no? Would he get bounced around from home to home, or would he be adopted by someone else? I would probably never know. Could I live with that? Would I regret my decision? I was the only family member he had that could rescue him.

I tried my best to ignore the yes I felt in my spirit until my husband finally spoke up. He said that we should say yes, but he said it with a "please don't be mad at me" expression on his face. Inside, I was throwing a massive temper tantrum, but I knew he was right. I hated that he was right! Being obedient to what I felt God was asking of us didn't mean I had to like it or even understand it. Maybe God was going to use us to change this little boy's future. Maybe everything would work out just fine. Sure, there was going to be challenges, but maybe it won't be as bad as my fear and imagination make it out to be. There was no way to know what was before us, but I knew the first step was saying, "Yes, I choose to trust You, Lord."

*****

We immediately began the foster care certification process. It was made clear to us that even though we were Thomas's aunt and uncle, we would still have to jump through all the hoops any other perspective adoptive parent would have to jump through. So our weeks became consumed by foster care certification classes, home studies, and family interviews. After a very long year, we were finally certified, and our home was approved and ready. We were told at this time that even though we were approved in our state, the state in which Thomas was living was not ready to release him to our custody.

After a few months of waiting, we received a phone call from the caseworker who told us that my half-brother's parental rights had been terminated. According to her, my brother broke into someone's home, ate their food, and then passed out on their couch where the owner later found him. He was probably homeless at the time—and apparently hungry enough to not think through the consequences. He was arrested and charged with breaking and entering. While he was in jail, the court took that opportunity to strip him of his parental rights.

Not long after that, we found out that Thomas's birth mother was in a new relationship. She had been attending all of her parenting classes and voluntarily agreed to have a breathalyzer placed in her home for random alcohol testing. She was staying clean and seemed to be getting her life in a stable place. She was participating in her weekly visits with Thomas, and the caseworker made it very clear to us that he could return to her custody if she continued to do well. At this point, nothing was guaranteed, but I knew that God would not have had us commit to the process if we were not supposed to adopt him. We had no choice but to continue to wait and see how everything played out.

*****

As we drove out of town heading to the small horse ranch, we were excited to finally be able to see Thomas and meet his foster family. Being able to visit him was a huge step forward, and we hadn't seen him since the houseboat vacation two years prior. He has been in the same foster home since he was taken into custody at twenty-one months old. I was hopeful that, with him being in the same home for that long, it was a good indication that he was doing well.

It isn't uncommon for children to be bounced around through multiple placements while they wait to be eligible for adoption.

We turned down the long gravel driveway kicking up dust in our wake. As we approached the house, we saw a boy in the front yard playing. The family must have heard us coming down the drive because a woman came outside. It looked like she was summoning the boy to follow her into the house. After a moment, she turned around and retreated back toward the door, and then out came her husband. They walked over to the boy together. I'm not exactly sure what happened between the time we unbuckled our seat belts and got out of the car, but they were wrestling the little boy to the ground. He was screaming and flailing wildly. It was an obvious struggle for them to restrain him long enough to carry him into the house against his will.

The woman met us at the door out of breath and very flustered. She introduced herself as the foster mother and then introduced her husband, who grunted a greeting and then quickly disappeared into another room, never to be seen again. She invited us to sit on the couch where Thomas was now sitting in what seemed to be a dazed stupor. It took me a moment to realize that he was awake. I found it odd that one minute he was screaming and being forcefully carried into the house, and the next minute he was sitting quietly on the couch. What in the world had just happened?

The foster mother took no time at all in telling us how terrible she thought Thomas was. She dove right in, neglecting any of the normal pleasantries. It was so immediate that it took both of us off guard. We had been told, for the past two years, that he was placed with an excellent foster family who had been caring for children for over thirty years with an impeccable reputation. If she was the gold standard, I couldn't even imagine what the families with bad reputations were like. She obviously hated him.

She started out by telling us that adopting Thomas would be a huge mistake. She had heard we had a daughter, and she was quick to say that we would be putting our daughter at risk. She said that he would rape her and probably burn down our home. She continued to share that he has a history of choking her animals and has done nothing but torment the other foster boy who was living with them.

According to her, he was an absolute terror. She no longer wanted him in her home. She made it clear that she wanted nothing more to do with him and was eagerly awaiting Children Services coming to remove him from her care. She followed that up with saying he was stupid. He didn't even know his colors or numbers, and he would grow up to be just like all the other Indians who end up drunk or dead in the gutter. She told us we would be absolute fools to adopt him.

I wasn't just shocked by the words that were coming out of her mouth but also by her tone of disgust. Her hatred was actually tangible. This whole time, he was sitting right next to me on the couch. If she was saying these things about him in front of strangers, what was she saying to him when no one else was around? I glanced over at him, and he seemed lethargic. I hoped he wasn't paying attention. What had he done that made her hate him so? Even if everything she was saying was true, he was only three years old. Teach him. Parent him. Love him. He seemed too young to be labeled so harshly. He couldn't possibly feel safe in her home.

Our meeting fueled the frustration I already felt toward the county. We had been begging them to go ahead and send him to us for the past two years, and here she was, begging to be done with him. We assured our caseworker many times that we would continue to do whatever they asked of us as foster parents until the adoption could be finalized. We had completed our certification process; we had three healthy and happy children already. They repeatedly assured us that he was in a safe and loving home with wonderful foster parents. That was obviously not the case. Either they were purposely lying to us, or she had somehow fooled them. She was obviously a pretty blunt person, so I figured the deception must lay with the caseworker.

Before we left her home, she walked us down the hallway so we could see Thomas's bedroom. His room had a bedframe, mattress, and a dresser. What his bedroom did not have were sheets, pillows, drapes over the window, closet doors, blankets, or toys of any kind.

The room was barren and cold. I just didn't understand. Had we stepped into some kind of foster-home twilight zone?

I wondered what we were getting ourselves into. Was she right? Was she just burnt out and bitter with the system? Was she crazy? We expected that adopting Thomas would have its difficulties. Our foster care training had taught us all about the trauma these children experience and their malbehaviors because of it, but seeing his situation firsthand was a bit shocking.

We drove back down the driveway with Thomas securely fastened in the back seat. I wish I could have taken him away from that home forever that day, but we were just there to visit and only had permission to keep him for one night. Christopher and I didn't speak as we drove away. I think we were just trying to process everything. We hadn't even pulled onto the main road before we heard a little voice from the back seat counting in a very defiant tone, "One... two...three...four..."

We smiled at each other when we realized that he was counting to prove her wrong. Maybe the things that she had just said about him weren't true. He did know his numbers, and he was making sure we knew it too. By the time we got back into town, he had moved on to his colors. He had been listening.

CHAPTER 3

The Lord will fight for you;
you need only to be still.
—Exodus 14:14

The following morning, we had an appointment scheduled to meet with the caseworker at her office. When we arrived, we were escorted into a large room where a panel of professionals had gathered. She instructed us to sit down, and a woman seated at the head of the table opened up the meeting. We thought we were just meeting with the caseworker. This was something entirely different and a little intimidating, not at all what we were expecting. A heads-up would have been nice.

One by one, they went around the room and introduced themselves. We were sitting before legal counsel for the county, Children's Services staff, a guardian ad litem, our caseworker, Thomas's foster mother, his therapist, and a departmental psychologist. After introductions, the floor was opened up for each person to share their thoughts on our adoption case.

They started with the foster mother, who adamantly expressed her concerns about Thomas being placed in our care just as she had to us the day before. She spoke of his disturbing behaviors and the threat she believed he posed to our family, specifically to our daughter. She said that she expected him to act out sexually and violently with her and with the other members of the family. She recommended he be placed in a home without other children.

She and Thomas's therapist seemed to be in cahoots as they began to feed off each other's comments and get more and more animated as they went. The therapist spoke of reactive attachment disorder, fetal alcohol syndrome, and his defiant behavior. She agreed that he should not be placed in our care but, when asked, did not have any other recommendations for placement.

We had just met Thomas's therapist at her office the previous day for one of his weekly sessions. During our visit, the therapist began to share Thomas's treatment plan with us in great detail. While she was speaking, Thomas began wandering the room picking up random items and bringing them to us. He brought us some clay he had been working with, a stuffed elephant, and a plastic caterpillar. As soon as we tried to engage him with an object, he would be gone in search of another.

We found ourselves piled high in toys, struggling to focus on the therapist's words. At one point, Thomas noticed that we were sitting next to a bookcase, so he decided to grab a book. He brought me a colorful book about animals. I opened it to show him the elephants, but after just one page, he was done and went off to grab another one. Each of the books was standing on end with only the spines showing. He didn't pause to read the titles. He just grabbed another one at random and brought it to me.

This next book was all white with black wording on the cover. He opened to a random page in the middle and pointed to the picture and made a questioning sound. It was a book with sketch drawings of a naked mom and dad. *Great*, I thought. He brought me a sex-ed book. He was waiting for a reply, so I told him that she was a mommy. Then he pointed to the other person, and I told him that he was a daddy. He seemed pleased enough with my answers, so he wandered away again in search of something else to bring me.

The therapist saw which book I was holding and immediately went into a panic. She started going on and on with the foster mother about how he must be sexualized. His book choice was a clear indication of sexual abuse! The level of escalation the therapist and the foster mother took the situation almost made me laugh out loud. I just thought, really, people? It was a book clearly chosen at random, and he was barely even interested in it.

My husband and I left her office that day believing the therapist was a complete loon, and here we sat in front of the panel, listening to her very alarming assessment of that event. Everything she was saying was said with so much drama and, what seemed to me, over-the-top exaggeration that I was sure that the panel wouldn't take her seriously. We had clearly witnessed two very different scenarios.

The caseworker was next, and she spoke very highly of us. She said she had some concerns but overall expressed her confidence that we would be a suitable placement for Thomas. She assured them that she had clearly communicated his issues and behaviors to us. By now, I was no longer confident that she had. He was being painted much more damaged than she had ever expressed to me during our many phone conversations. I was starting to wonder if I had been deceived or simply failed to grasp the severity of the situation.

I hoped that her statements would carry a little more weight since she was the only one there who actually knew us, but as they continued taking statements around the room, it was clear to me that we were not the panel's choice. I was so confused. We had done everything they had asked of us, and now we were hearing that they didn't approve of us. They clearly didn't intend to let us adopt him. What had we been doing for the past year and a half? For the first time, I feared that they would deny our petition to adopt.

The guardian ad litem was the last one to speak. I didn't even know what a guardian ad litem was, but he requested to speak to us in private before he entered his vote into the record. We followed him to a conference room, and he began by explaining to us that he was Thomas's attorney. He was there to advocate for Thomas and no one else. He asked us a few questions about ourselves and our family, but I don't remember either of us saying anything particularly inspiring or insightful.

Then he asked us what it would mean if we were told that we couldn't adopt him. Neither one of us answered right away as we paused to consider the question. Then my eyes filled with tears, and my heart sank. I was surprised at the flood of emotion I was feeling. Thomas was mine! He already belonged in our family. We had made room for him physically and, apparently, emotionally as well. That's when I knew that God had truly changed my heart. I looked at Christopher, and his eyes were full of tears too. When we expressed how we felt and how heartbroken we would be, he closed his file, got up from the table, and told us to wait until someone came for us.

We waited nervously for about an hour. I felt that our future was in his hands. Was he against us or for us? He didn't give us any indication either way before he left the room, but we believed he went to plead our case. I wondered how much his voice would really matter when the majority of the panel had already voted against us. My stomach was in knots. My mind was reviewing our answers, wondering if we had said or done anything wrong.

Finally, we were called back into the room. The woman in charge of the proceeding told us that after a long deliberation, they had approved us for placement. A complete about-face! I would have liked to have been a fly on the wall to know what had happened during that hour-long conversation. What we had said to the attorney must have worked. It must have been enough to assure him that Thomas would be in good hands if they allowed us to have him. Somehow he had to have persuaded the whole panel to change their minds. I'm sure that was no easy feat.

*****

Before we returned home, we were told that Thomas's birth mother was voluntarily surrendering her parental rights. She was newly married and pregnant again. Having an open case with Children Services while you are pregnant means that the unborn child will be automatically taken into custody as soon as it is born. If you are deemed unfit to raise the children you already have, they will not allow you to raise the next one either. In effort for her to continue to stabilize her life and move forward, she chose to surrender her parental rights of Thomas and officially close her case so that she could keep her unborn child.

We met with her and a representative from her tribal government. Thomas's birth mother is Native American, which means that the tribe has a direct investment over the placement of her children. In the past, so many Native American children were being adopted out to Caucasian families without any tribal involvement. Those children were losing all connection to their people group and to their unique traditions. Laws have since been passed to protect the heritage of these sovereign nations by giving them the legal right to step in and stop any adoptive placement involving their people. They can overrule any state decisions for a minor child at any time, even after they have been legally adopted. It was imperative that we receive the tribe's blessing.

Fortunately for us, Thomas's birth mother wanted us to adopt him. Since her tribe tracks their genealogy through the mother and not the father, her blessing was very influential. Since she grew up in the tribe's foster care system, she put a stipulation on her surrender that said that Thomas would have to remain outside of their social system. She claimed that she was emotionally and sexually abused for much of her teenage years, and she did not want that for Thomas. She felt that the United States' foster care system had more regulations and oversight.

For the tribe to honor her request, Christopher and I had to provide our lineage so that they could confirm that any Native American ancestors of ours were not from warring tribes. I hadn't realized that tribes could still be at war with one another, or at least held concerns that Thomas could fall into enemy hands. Once all of that was settled, we had finally received the last piece necessary to move forward with the adoption.

*****

We returned home without Thomas, but we were assured that it wouldn't be much longer. All we had to do now was wait—again. We didn't realize that our wait would not end until right before his fifth birthday. Almost three years after that first initial phone call. Someone filed a statement with the agency that my brother was not actually the biological father. This turned into an investigation that led them to another man that the caseworker says looks just like Thomas.

She was completely convinced that this other man was the biological father, but they were unable to locate him for paternity testing. My brother refused to be tested. So by law, the agency had to place an ad in the local newspaper imploring this man to contact them. They had to run the ad for six months and hope for a response. He eventually contacted them, but he refused to be involved. Then they had to find that man's extended family and ask each of them if they were interested, and they said they were not. Officially, paternity has never been established for Thomas, but my brother's name is on the original birth certificate, making me his legal aunt. Our adoption petition stood once again.

That whole process took most of a year. All the while, Thomas was still with the foster mother who hated him and didn't want him. She had been requesting to have him removed from her home long before we met her. She eventually came to a point where she was no longer willing to wait. She put all of his belongings into trash bags and dumped him off in the agency's lobby. There were no caseworkers there at the time because they were all out of the building visiting clients, so Thomas sat in the lobby alone for a few hours until someone returned to receive him.

The caseworker called us to let us know what had happened and that Thomas had been placed with a new foster family. It was only then that she informed us that he had thrown a tantrum, kicked his headboard, and had broken his leg (according to the foster mother). He was in a cast, and by the way, he also had cigarette burns on his body. I have two rambunctious boys. I know that it doesn't always take much to break a bone, but leg bones are pretty strong. That must have been some tantrum. That left us wondering if the abuse caused his behavior or if his behavior spurned the abuse; either way, inexcusable. I'd probably throw a tantrum too if you burned me with cigarettes.

Thomas was placed with a very nice Mormon family who had other special needs children of varying ages. They offered to adopt him if we changed our minds, but we hadn't. God had clearly told us to adopt him, so our minds had been set for years. After he was with this new foster family for three months, we received a call that the time had finally come for me to go get him with the stipulation that my husband not accompany me. The caseworker told me that men were children abusers, so he was forbidden from joining me, even if we paid his own way. It seemed like everything and everyone had been working against us, but we were thankful and thrilled to finally be able to bring him home even though my husband couldn't join me.

The new foster mother was very kind to Thomas and helped prepare him as much as she could for his new "forever home." Once we were given permission to contact him by phone, she encouraged him to start calling us mom and dad. We mailed him an adoption book full of pictures of us, his new home, and his new brothers and sister. Each of them had drawn him pictures and wrote him notes of how excited they were to have him join the family.

We had been talking to them about Thomas for years now. A caseworker had even interviewed each one of them separately, asking how they felt about a new brother joining the family all the way back at the beginning of this process. They were aware from the very start, but three years is an eternity when you're that young. All we had to show them during that time was a few photographs of him from the houseboat trip. He had become their distant, elusive sibling.

Family and friends celebrated with us when we shared the news. Christmas was a month away, and I was scheduled to pick him up in a matter of days. We were excited to be able to celebrate the holiday together as a whole family. We couldn't wait to close this long chapter of our lives. We never would have thought that it was going to take three years to get him or that we would experience so many ups and downs in the process. I was thankful that we were not going to start another year separated from each other and that we could finally begin the new year as a family.

CHAPTER 4

When I am afraid, I will put my trust in you.
—Psalm 56:3

Bringing an older child into your home instantly changes everything. With a newborn, you have time to gradually adjust to their growing personality and to allow it to infuse into the daily workings of the family. When you adopt an older child, their personality is well established, and they enter your home with vastly different expectations and life experiences. If they are coming out of the foster care system, they have already experienced a great deal of uncertainty and have undoubtedly experienced some level of trauma in their lives.

I spent those first few weeks observing Thomas very closely. I had no idea what he did or did not know, or the extent of his developmental delays and how those affected him. He was extremely quiet and stoic, so it was difficult to know what he was thinking or feeling. Any questions I asked were usually met with a blank stare. I couldn't tell if he didn't understand the question or if he just didn't want to answer me. Maybe he didn't know how to respond. Occasionally, there might be a tilt of his head or a subtle shoulder shrug, but if you weren't watching him closely, you could easily miss it.

It would have been easier if I would have known some basic things about him such as his favorite color or his favorite food, but as the days went by, I wasn't convinced that anyone had taken the time to discover those things about him. I wasn't sure if he even knew those things about himself. His previous home didn't seem like it was an environment that fostered any kind of growth and discovery. Overall, Thomas was an enigma to me. I felt like I was given a pile of puzzle pieces without the picture on the box, and I had to blindly figure out how the pieces fit together.

There were obvious gaps with some of the basic things he should have been taught or been capable of doing by the age of four or five. By now, there should have been plenty of verbal communication happening, but in Thomas's case, there was virtually no communication at all, so the depth of his cognitive understanding was a mystery to me. The few words he did speak were pronounced incorrectly. He left off the first letter or consonant of most of his words, where *fishy* was pronounced *-ishy*.

Complex words were even more difficult for him. Since he came to live with us in December, the home was abuzz with Christmas. He pronounced Christmas as "grimp-us," which just tickled the other children. They tried incessantly to correct his pronunciation. He just couldn't hear the difference between his pronunciation and the way anyone else was saying it. He spent that first year with us in speech therapy so that he could learn how to make the sounds he was missing.

It was immediately evident that Thomas was grossly behind in his vocabulary and comprehension skills because he was often confused by the conversations happening around him. He generally assumed that he was being spoken about, even if he wasn't the topic of conversation. If there was conversational laughter, he usually believed he was being made fun of, which made him angry. Most of the time, he didn't engage in anything having to do with anyone else. He seemed to be used to going it alone or occupying his time in his own little world.

He went through many of the developmental milestones you would expect from a one- or two-year-old within the first few months. We took that as an indication that he was catching up to his peers and showing signs of stabilizing. I will admit that the stripping stage was a little awkward for everyone.

He thought it was hilarious to shake his little naked body no matter where we were or who was around. We had to constantly remind him to remain dressed. It would have probably been seen as cute or funny if he was still a toddler, but with him just turning five, it was a rather odd and inappropriate thing to do. At least he was finding some sense of freedom to be silly.

His overall behavior was quite strange, and I couldn't understand a lot of what he would do. He wandered around the house aimlessly and fidgeted all the time. His communication and body language were generally confusing and nonsensical. He would often stop and stare off into space. Not the relaxing mind-shut-down thing that we can all do when we're relaxing or daydreaming, but more like a skip in the record where you just stop however you were in that moment.

It seemed that no one had taken the time to teach him how to conduct himself appropriately. Behavioral modification is very important for the development of a small child. Those early years is when they are taught how to control their bodies, use their words, share, say *please* and *thank you*, how to be considerate of others, and how to appropriately express their emotions. He didn't seem to be aware of any of those basic social constructs.

There are naturally going to be different expectations set from one home to another. Every family develops its own flow and acceptable social behavior, whether it is intentionally taught or only taught by example. Morality, religion, political views, traditions, birth order, along with the culmination of a shared history all play a part in how each person behaves and functions within a family.

One particular behavior that is valued in one family may not be a big deal in another. In some homes, words like *stupid* or *sucks* are considered just as wrong to say as a curse word would be to another family. So naturally, I expected there to be some differences between our home and the home that Thomas had been accustomed to. He lived with them for almost three years. It was really all that he knew, but I could never pinpoint a baseline of what he was taught or not taught.

From what little I observed from that foster family, combined with the behaviors I was seeing day after day, it seemed like he had been living in more of a holding pattern. Instead of integrating him into a temporary family setting and teaching him family life, I can only assume that he was just cared for in the most basic sense. He was fed. He had a place to sleep, but it didn't seem like it went beyond that—at least not since we had met them.

He seemed to be the product of not being parented at all. It was clear to me that he was accustomed to doing whatever he felt was right in the moment, and he didn't have any real fear or concern with being corrected or given a consequence. Maybe they tried to really care for him and help him at first but didn't know how or didn't have the perseverance to work through his issues. Who knows?

His foster mother told me once that she just gave in to whatever he wanted whenever he screamed and threw a fit because it was easier than dealing with him. She said it didn't make a difference if they were at home or in public; she didn't bother trying to teach him to stop. If he wanted a toy, she bought it. If he wanted candy, she gave it to him. Basically, she inadvertently taught him to tantrum his way through life.

I think she had made up her mind somewhere along the way that he just wasn't worth her investment. In her mind, she had already determined his fate. By the time I met her, she wasn't interested in helping him in any capacity. Her frustration had festered into hatred. She had wanted to be done with him for years, and she seemed to have been simply dealing with him day after day until she could finally be rid of him.

*****

What foster children allow to go in and out of their bodies is the one thing that they can have absolute control over. They have been unable to control where they live or who they live with, but they can control what they eat and when they go to the toilet. It isn't uncommon for them to sneak food, hide food, binge food, or refuse to even eat food. Thomas was no exception. He refused to eat just about everything we fed him except macaroni and cheese and SpaghettiOs and, of course, candy.

If there was a holiday or a party with candy, he ate every piece he could get his little hands on, even if it was given to someone else. He would eat his own as quickly as possible, and then he would sneak into his siblings' bedrooms and eat theirs as well. He was terrible at covering up his tracks though. We would find wrappers all over his room: in his bed, under his mattress, in his pillowcase, stuffed into and under toys, and even into a little hole he had created in the plaster wall next to his bed. Of course, he would adamantly deny that he had eaten the candy even while we would be shaking empty wrappers out of his pillowcase.

We quickly discovered that denial was his go to response. I started asking him why he didn't just throw the wrappers in the trash can because then it would actually be deniable, but my husband was quick to stop me so that I didn't inadvertently teach him how to sneak better. His inability to hide what he was doing was working to our advantage.

It was his lack of self-control and his binging behavior that caused me to be aware of what foods I was buying and where I was storing it. I had to change the way I was shopping. Eventually, I went from buying a week or two of groceries at a time to shopping almost on a daily basis so that I could control his consumption.

If I purchased snacks like fruit gummies, snack cakes, crackers, cookies, or yogurt, they would disappear almost immediately. Whole unopened bags of chips and boxes of crackers or snack cakes would be emptied overnight. I started finding assorted food wrappers shoved between the couch cushions. Things that were meant to last a week or more would be gone within hours. I either hid things, or I just stopped buying them altogether. His older brother, Isaiah, harbored a great deal of unforgiveness toward Thomas for years simply because he distinctly remembers that all of his favorite foods disappeared after he came to live with us. He felt robbed.

Christopher started getting out of bed and walking the house at random times during the night because we knew Thomas would be up and about rummaging around. He liked to pillage the pantry and then watch television or wander the house, getting into the other children's belongings while they slept. Whenever he would hear Dad coming, he would panic and leave whatever it was he was sneaking right where he had been, which usually meant that the TV screen was left on to shine in the darkness.

Thomas would race to his bed and close his eyes as tightly as he could and pretend that he had been peacefully sleeping there all along. Whenever we've tried to stir him to speak to him, he would yawn and respond all groggy as if we had woken him from a dream. He was a masterful pretender who honestly believed he was outsmarting us. After all, there was always another sibling he could blame for the missing food or the inevitable mess he left behind.

On occasion, he would find himself blocked and unable to make it back to his bedroom without being confronted. Whenever that happened, he would hide in the shadows with his eyes tightly closed, thinking that if he couldn't see us, then he couldn't be seen at all. He would remain unmoved, even when his father would approach him and start speaking directly to him by name. There he would remain, just like a statue. This cat and mouse continued night after night after night. Thomas would be so exhausted come morning that he would refuse to get out of bed for school and then become angry with us when we insisted.

During the day, he would often hide in the bathroom for long periods of time. I think he was mostly doing that to get away from us, but it took him leaving an empty bottle of grated parmesan cheese and a bag of half-eaten grapes behind the toilet for us to figure out that he was also using it as a way to sneak food. I just kept thinking, there was a trash can right there. Why won't he use the stinking trash cans? When we would ask him to quit sneaking and eating in the bathroom because the bathroom was just too dirty of a place for food, he would maintain a blank look on his face as if he had absolutely no idea what you were even talking about.

Reasoning with him was impossible, so we would just clean up his mess, change how we hid things, and tried to move on. We discussed locking up the refrigerator and the cabinets, but all that would do was inconvenience and punish everyone else. I was convinced that locking things up would have just provided him with one more challenge to overcome and would have resulted in broken handles and busted locks. So we just changed what we could and dealt with the rest. I was hopeful that, in time, he would realize that he was safe and that he didn't have to sneak around and avoid us all the time.

*****

Even as the months went by, Thomas remained in a constant state of hypervigilance and never seemed to settle into a restful state of being. The most basic everyday events caused him to panic. The world was a terrifying place for him. It didn't seem like the people who had been entrusted with his care affirmed him or shown him any kind of affection. His behavior was that of a child who had only known abuse and didn't have any sense of safety or security. Fear had become his constant companion.

Remembering his love for water, I would often run a bath for him to play in so that he could relax, but when it came to washing his hair or rinsing the soap off his body, he was absolutely terrified. He would claw and fight me as if I was trying to drown him. Sometimes it was necessary for us to have him shower instead; Thomas behaved as though the water hitting his skin caused him physical pain. He would avoid it by standing in the very back of the shower, and then he would flinch whenever I touched him to wash his body. He would howl in anguish each time I had to pull him under the water to rinse off the soap. His whole body would literally convulse.

I don't know what his foster family had done to him, but his reaction, combined with the scars from the cigarette burns that were all over his body, broke my heart and made me furious all at the same time. Sure, he had been neglected by his birth parents. They were not equipped to adequately care for him, but this level of trauma didn't come from either of them. This trauma came from the foster family. They had to have been beating him on a regular basis with the way he responded to anything that touched his body.

Thomas rejected any sort of physical contact from everyone, especially with me being the mother figure. His foster mother, case manager, and therapist were all middle-aged white women. His birth mother is Native American. Unconsciously, he trusts darker-skinned women more and automatically distrusts paler-skinned women. The white women kept him away from the only one who he felt truly loved him and who he felt a natural connection to. Through the filter of his experiences, I would think that most children in his situation would hold the same prejudice.

I just wanted to be able to touch him, hug him, and snuggle with him the way that I could with my other children, but he always remained outside of my reach. If I put him on my lap, he quickly slid off and wandered away. He avoided sitting anywhere near me. If he wanted to walk past me, he did so cautiously and as far from my reach as possible, even if that meant pressing himself against the wall to do so. If I tried to hug him, he would push on me and wiggle himself free. He had a clear aversion to women, but he didn't seem to know what to do with my husband. He didn't seem to have much experience around men.

Over time, I expected him to become more comfortable with the family and for some of those avoidance behaviors to fade away. I expected our daily interactions to become easier and more natural, but they never did. I was never able to break through his protective barrier. Thomas had frequent night terrors, but he didn't speak of them or seek anyone out for any kind of comfort like his siblings would have done. He dealt with them on his own, and if we heard him stirring and went to him, our presence only seemed to make his distress worse.

It was clear to me that he has never been consistently nurtured or comforted. He would much rather pretend to be okay or even asleep then gain any of our attention. Thomas instead found comfort in his blankets. They seemed to provide a security for him that he wasn't able to receive from people. He would bury himself in them even if it was eighty degrees and his body was covered in sweat. They became his protective barrier from the world.

On our first grocery trip together, we went to the canned goods aisle to choose some vegetables for dinner. He wouldn't speak to me, but he was following me through the store and kept busy by watching the other shoppers. When I reached out to grab a can of green beans off the shelf, Thomas hit the floor. When I looked down to see what had happened, he was cowering and looking up at me with his hands in front of his face. He had expected me to strike him. I tried to assure him I was only reaching for the can, but the more I spoke to him, the more panic he displayed. The only thing I could do was to ignore him and continue shopping and hope that, over time, he would discover that I wasn't going to hurt him.

It took over a year for him to stop flinching or hitting the floor whenever I would move around him. I had to learn to be very slow and deliberate with my movements. I did my best to warn him before I needed to touch him for any reason. So as you can imagine, dressing him was a constant struggle because it required a lot of touching on my part. I would often have to chase him down or dress him piece by piece over a longer period of time. Dressing and bathing became a dreaded part of my day. He preferred to live in his pajamas, even after he wet his bed and soaked himself. Having to remove all of his clothes to bathe him and then strip and wash his bedding was such a struggle for him, especially if his blanket needed washing as well.

There were many strange behaviors that communicated his heightened level of stress and constant anxiety. He was always chewing on his fingers. His nails would be chewed down so far that they would bleed. Even with our constant discouragement, he continued to hide under his blankets and chew on his toenails. He also picked at absolutely everything. He would peel the soles off of his shoes in a matter of days. He would pick at our plaster walls until they started to crumble. If there was a loose stitch, he would pull and unravel whatever it was attached to.

He would deliberately shred his jeans, rip holes in his socks, and chew holes in his shirts while he was wearing them. Then he would become upset that his clothes and shoes were in tatters. He would expect an immediate replacement. If we didn't rush out and replace them right away, he took it as a personal rejection and would then tell the neighbors that we neglect and abuse him, or that we were so poor we couldn't afford to buy him nice things. That was never the case.

He was especially particular with his shoes. His shoes that would only be a week or two old would look like he had been wearing them for months. Although he was the cause of his shoes being so tattered, he expected to have a new pair at his bidding, which I generally refused to provide. It escalated as he got older, and his classmates began to make fun of him for it. He would come home furious with me that he didn't have the nice, expensive shoes like they had. Since he destroyed everything so quickly, I usually shopped at discount stores. Shoes became a huge source of contention between us.

For me, it wasn't about the shoes. It was about the disregard and lack of appreciation for the things that were given to him. It was the expectation that he could do whatever he wanted, and the world had to accommodate and serve him. Shoes just happened to become our battleground. It was the mountain that I refused to die upon. He was told over and over again that as soon as he respected his shoes, stopped shredding them up, and proved that he could keep them in good condition for more than a week or two, I would consider going to the mall to buy him a more expensive pair.

Being told that he had to do something first before he got what he wanted infuriated him, and we fought about it continually. By the way he acted, you would have thought I never bought him shoes when, in reality, he received a new pair every few weeks. Two or three times more often than the other children got them. He destroyed them so quickly that I had to keep extras hidden in my bedroom just in case. We never knew when his soles would be hanging on by a thread, and another pair would be needed just so we could leave the house.

One morning, the kids and I were rushing out the door for school. I told Thomas it was time to leave, but he just stood by the door, unmoving. I asked him why he wasn't getting in the car, and he said that he couldn't because he didn't have any shoes to wear. Of course, he did, so I asked him where he had put them the night before. He said that he didn't know. They were just gone. I told him to grab another pair, but he said he couldn't. When I asked him why, he said they were *all* gone—every single pair.

I had just checked all of his shoes two days prior when he had asked me for a new pair. They were looking a bit worn, but for Thomas, they were still in excellent condition and completely functional so I told him it would be a little while before we went shoe shopping again. Now all of a sudden, he was telling me he couldn't go to school because he didn't own any shoes. I rushed around looking in all his usual hiding places while he waited by the door. I even checked the trash cans outside where he has been known to throw them away.

He thought that if all of his shoes were gone, then I would have no choice but to buy him the expensive pair that he wanted from the mall. What he didn't think through though was that the mall wasn't open at seven o'clock in the morning on a Tuesday. The only place open that early in the morning was Walmart, the very store he didn't want shoes from. He thought he had outsmarted me, and he had won the war. To his shock and horror, I took him to Walmart in his socks where I forced him to select a new pair. He was so furious with me that he refused to speak to me or even look in my direction. I dropped him off at school as usual.

A few months later, I was outside trimming a large bush on the side of our house. As I bent down to clean up the clippings, I noticed something. Wouldn't you know that hidden under that bush was one of the pairs of shoes I had searched for that morning? I never found the others, but it confirmed what I already knew to be true. He had tried to force my hand. What he has failed to realized is that those sorts of tactics only make me more determined than ever to hold my ground.

CHAPTER 5

Love is patient, love is kind and is not jealous.
—1 Corinthians 13:4

We were assigned a new caseworker with Children Services when Thomas came to live with us. She was nice and engaging and came to our home every month for that first year to help us transition through the foster-to-adopt process. We found out that we were not allowed to adopt him right away. We had to foster him for at least twelve months so that Children's Services could be assured that all was well, and we weren't going to tell them to take him away.

The caseworker asked us with each visit if we were still planning to adopt him. I didn't understand why she kept asking us that same question. We took Thomas for the sole purpose of adopting him. We were only fostering him because they told us that we had no choice. Apparently, giving a child back was an option. Neither one of us knew that at the time. I kept wondering if she was forgetting our answer, or maybe she was testing our commitment. We both felt like giving him back would reflect negatively on us. That we didn't have what it takes, that we weren't seriously committed. After three years of fighting to get him, hadn't we proven our resolve?

We didn't realize that adoptions could fail or that families could change their minds. Once the papers were signed and I picked him up, we thought that was that. We would never think to contribute further to his trauma and abandonment issues by sending him back into the very system that broke him in the first place. We knew that we knew that God had asked us to adopt him. As far as we were concerned, it was a done deal as far back as that first phone call asking if we would consider taking him.

Going into it, Christopher and I thought we had a clear understanding of how challenging adopting Thomas was going to be. We attended three months of foster care classes that spelled out the issues and behaviors foster children display. We had already experienced all of them, and we weren't shocked by them. Even in the chaos, we felt like we were making some progress.

We had taken the time to study early childhood development and trauma. We knew that you couldn't unravel years in a matter of months. We expected it to take time. We were very hopeful. We believed that a stable home with a loving mother and father would, over time, bring a security and safety to Thomas that would ultimately make way for the emotional healing he so desperately needed. He just needed a chance, and we were willing to give that to him.

We both expected that his behaviors would slowly fade away and that a new identity would eventually form. I believed that he would come to understand how we had chosen him and fought for him in ways we never had to fight for our other children. We were positive that it would all work out. With God, we could do anything. We were hopeful that one day Thomas would be able to say, "Thank you for adopting me." Or even, "I love you." Maybe we were just fooling ourselves. Maybe we were too naïve.

*****

Unfortunately, that initial excitement that our children had toward Thomas faded pretty quickly. The fantasy of having a new brother to play with did not match up with reality. Conflict was to be expected as the four of them learned how to adjust to one another, but Thomas didn't have any idea of how to get along with other children. He was very quick to hit, bite, or cuss at them to get his way.

Whenever the older children were really angry with one another, they might call one another *dummy, stupid,* or even say, "I hate you." Those statements alone incited the receiver to tears and resulted in devastated emotions. So as you can imagine, they were utterly shocked at the way Thomas was speaking to them. They had been taught their whole lives that those types of behaviors were wrong, and here comes their new brother breaking all the rules and violating what they knew to be right.

Our once peaceful home seemed to turn into a war zone almost overnight. Our older children were suddenly living with an enemy who seemed set on causing destruction. So much of my energy was spent on damage control and navigating all the unknown land mines of parenting a child like Thomas. He operated in such contrast to the rest of us that it never crossed my mind to anticipate some of the things he would do. He seemed to thrive on creating chaos, and it put a limit on what we could do, where we could go, and whom we would allow him to be around.

One of the few social situations we allowed Thomas to be in outside of preschool was church on Sunday mornings. Whenever he would be dropped off in the children's class, he would stand back quietly to observe the dynamics of the room. What he lacked in verbal and cognitive ability, he made up for in the way he could read a social situation. That was the survival instinct of a foster child coming out. Once he got a read on the room, watch out! Within minutes, he would have singled out a target, moved in, punched them, and taken whatever they were playing with right out of their hands.

Asking to have a turn or even waiting until the other child was done didn't seem to cross his mind. I'm not sure if it really had anything to do with the actual toy or just the fact that he decided he could take them out easily enough. It was impressive how quickly he could turn a whole room of children against him. Because of that, we rarely left him with a sitter, and we couldn't trust him to have a playdate or a sleepover under any circumstances for years.

I spent a lot of time denying Thomas his independence, but until he could show me that he could listen and control himself, it just wasn't beneficial for him or anyone else. He couldn't see the problems he was causing, and I was not going to subject other children or adults to his behavior. He didn't respond to normal correction or function within typical parental expectations. Some of our friends and family thought we were crazy whenever we shared some of our experiences with them or when we would not allow him to have the same freedoms as his siblings. Unless you experience it yourself, it's hard to explain and fully understand.

When Thomas came to live with us, my husband and I were pastoring and growing a new church plant in our hometown. Our congregation was growing, and our lives were consumed with all sorts of meetings and gatherings that we typically hosted in our home. It wasn't uncommon for us to have fifty to one hundred people in our house at a time. There were plenty of adults around, and with such a tight-knit community, all of us helped parent one another's children. Even though there were plenty of ways to get noticed, Thomas managed to keep himself under the radar for a time.

It took everyone a while to catch on to the things he was doing. You really had to watch him, and watch him very closely. He could pinch or bite another child so quickly without ever making a sound or even changing his face expression. It really was impressive. He would wait to strike until the adults would glance away, and then all of a sudden, another child would be crying, but nothing would have appeared to have happened. Although most of his attacks he executed away from the watchful eyes of the adults, it wasn't unheard of for him to hurt someone right in the middle of a crowded room and no one witness it.

As expected, the other children started tattling on him constantly. It was evident that he was cursing at them and hurting them repeatedly. I spent many of our church meetings going up and down the stairs dealing with one conflict after another. Children would be crying; toys were getting broken. The whole upstairs would be in an uproar. The constant interruptions and nonstop fighting was exhausting.

It was very difficult to stay present and to focus on a prayer meeting taking place when I could hear the ruckus happening right above me. Sometimes after mediating a conflict, I wouldn't even make it back downstairs to my seat before having to turn around to deal with something else he's done. The other parents were often right there with me, trying to discern the situation and then discipline or console their own little ones.

If we ever hoped to restore some order in our home, we needed to find the root cause of Thomas's behaviors and try our best to correct them—and quickly. Years of behaving one way isn't easily undone, but if we could understand the thought process behind it, I figured we had a better chance of correcting it. A lot of times, it just seemed like Thomas was hurting the other children just for the pleasure of seeing their reaction. I've caught glimpses of a sinister smile cross his face after he had inflicted pain on someone. You could catch it for the briefest of moments before he would rein it in and hide it. How do you begin to correct that?

Most of Thomas's behaviors seemed to stem from jealousy. If one of his siblings liked something, he was sure to steal it, smash it, or throw it away. Our oldest son, Jacob, loved Legos, and he would spend hours crafting elaborate designs that were proudly displayed on his bookcase. He made Lego cars, houses, and spaceships, all to precise specifications. Thomas would wait for the perfect opportunity and then sneak into Jacob's bedroom and smash one of them on the floor.

When confronted, Thomas would portray complete ignorance as to what could have possibly happened. According to him, he never did anything wrong, ever. Denial was the go-to response to absolutely everything. He was always innocent. Jacob would be so devastated. Eventually, he started taking matters into his own hands. He figured he might as well go ahead and retaliate and get some of his anger out because he knew Thomas was going to cry and say that he hit him even if he didn't. It seemed like natural consequences to me, so I rarely interfered.

Eventually, Thomas stopped smashing the Lego creations because he figured out that I wasn't going to stop Jacob from confronting and hitting him in return. I always made sure Jacob didn't take it too far, and somewhere along the way, Thomas decided he didn't want to get punched anymore. So instead of smashing them, he started stealing the specialty pieces that were crucial to completing the designs. We quickly discovered that if something wasn't working out for Thomas one way, he just reformulated a new attack strategy.

We noticed that other things started disappearing as well. We had to learn to check the trash cans whenever we couldn't find something, but the missing items could turn up anywhere. Sometimes they were in Thomas's bed hidden under his mattress, in his pillowcase, or wrapped up in his blankets. Other times we would find things in the backyard under rocks, bushes, and even up in the tree branches. Sometimes we would find them right away, and other times we wouldn't find them for months. Some things never turned back up again.

Thomas popped the heads off our daughter's Barbie dolls and snapped off her horse's legs—anything he noticed that she cherished. He would come to me crying saying that his sister bit him, but somehow the teeth marks on his arm always matched his own mouth perfectly. Most of his attentions were not focused toward his sister, but she never completely escaped his wrath. No one did. He focused most of his attentions toward our middle son, Isaiah. We believe it was because he has a similar look to the foster boy that Thomas lived with for many years, but whatever the reason, he clearly targeted Isaiah the most.

Thomas would try to get him in trouble multiple times in a day by making up scenarios that couldn't have possibly happened. For instance, one winter day, I was sitting on the couch sharing a blanket with Isaiah while we watched a movie together. At the top of the stairs, Thomas started screaming, "Stop it! Stop it! You're hurting me!" Then he started screaming his brother's name, and then he actually flung himself down the stairs. Our stairs were very steep and, luckily for him, carpeted. He didn't just fall down the stairs. He tumbled head over heels all the way to the bottom with complete commitment. I know it had to hurt because it was a terribly painful thing to witness.

When I went to him and asked him how his brother could have pushed him down the stairs when he was sitting with me on the couch, he continued to cry and say that Isaiah had done it. No matter what evidence I presented him that was contrary to his own account, he had somehow utterly convinced himself that his brother had pushed him down those stairs. No amount of reason ever made a difference. He would then spend the rest of the day flinching and crying around Isaiah as if the incident had really happened just as he claimed.

On another occasion, Thomas was upstairs playing alone. Isaiah was at a friend's house for the weekend, and the house was relatively quiet. All of a sudden, I heard Thomas screaming and crying. When I got to the bottom of the steps to see what was happening, Thomas was standing at the top of the staircase punching himself in the face and then slamming himself into the wall.

I just stood there watching him. He didn't notice me, so he continued to scream and punch himself over and over again. His face had turned bright red, and tears were streaming down his cheeks. I finally spoke up and asked him what in the world he was doing. He told me that Isaiah had just beaten him up, the same brother who wasn't even home.

These types of scenarios became a regular occurrence. He threw himself down the stairs often enough that we stopped reacting to it. He never could understand why we didn't believe him, and he genuinely felt betrayed and violated by our disbelief. He never changed any of his stories or believed anything differently than what he had fabricated in his own mind. It was bewildering. It took a couple of years for him to realize that he wasn't getting anywhere by hurting himself, and eventually he stopped.

Whenever Thomas wasn't resorting to such drastic measures to get the others in trouble, he was instigating conflicts within everyday life. He would get everyone so riled up that I would often have to separate each of them to try to make sense of what had happened. Finding the truth in four different accounts of the same situation was near impossible, especially when emotions were high.

There was a definite buildup of hurt and resentment toward Thomas that caused the others to gang up against him from time to time. I knew even in those instances that he was ultimately the instigator. If he wasn't treating them the way he was, the others wouldn't have had to join forces against him in the first place. In the end, everyone played their part though, and Thomas ultimately won. He had successfully ruined whatever peace and enjoyment that had been happening in that moment. I would then have to go around one by one, addressing everyone's contribution to the conflict.

It was a challenge to teach my older boys that just because someone says something terrible to you doesn't mean you have the right to say hurtful things in return; or if they break your toy, you should go break theirs. One evil should not be paid back with another evil, and sinning in your own anger is never okay. Teaching them biblical principles in the midst of constant combat was very difficult for them to grasp. Inevitably, all of them would end up upset with me—Thomas, because I was singling him out and punishing him for things he didn't do, and the others because they felt an overall sense of injustice.

Even though it was not my intention at all, the older boys felt that they were being punished if they were redirected, separated, or received any kind of correction. In their minds, it was yet another way Thomas was getting away with whatever it was he was doing. Thomas never got away with anything. You just couldn't teach him or reason with him. No amount of punishment or consequence seemed to change anything. They never felt that Thomas got what he deserved. What they were really upset about was that his punishments never incited repentance or remorse and that he would continue the same behavior a moment later, sometimes with even more malice and vengefulness than before. In truth, they just didn't like him.

CHAPTER 6

Children, obey your parents in
the Lord, for this is right.
—Ephesians 6:1

Over time, Thomas settled in and realized that the caseworker wasn't there to take him away with every visit and that he was where he was staying. She seemed to be pleased with his progress, so I didn't find his escalating behaviors particularly alarming. After all, you tend to show your ugly side once you start getting comfortable. I took that as a baby step in the right direction. The ugly needed to be revealed if there was any hope of correcting or healing it.

It hadn't taken us long to learn his ways, and we knew that Thomas would deny everything he did no matter the circumstance, so we stopped asking him if he did it at all. Behavior modification became my daily focus. Fortunately for us, Christopher and I have never really had any issues with parenting as a team. We were generally on the same page with discipline, and we endeavored to never undermine each other. Of course, we failed from time to time, usually on my end, but we had established clear expectations and consequences with our older three long before Thomas came along.

If we told one of them to stop something, we expected them to obey; and if they didn't, there was an immediate response from one of us. We never threatened to punish without following through, and we never resorted to counting and waiting for compliance. We have a family mantra that each one of our children can still recite to this day without missing a beat. If I ask them how they should obey, they respond with, "Right away, all the way, and in a happy way."

Basically, that reminds them that Dad and Mom are the established authority in their lives, so we are always in charge. Whenever we ask them to do something, we expect them to obey us right away. Not when they want to or only when they feel like getting around to it. All the way means that half-obedience is not obedience at all. They do not have the right to pick and choose what part of my instructions they follow. If I tell them to stop running and to sit down and they only stop running, then they did not obey all the way.

The last one can be the hardest because if they obey with a happy heart, that means that they can't mumble under their breath as they walk away, throw things, slam doors, or complain about it whenever they have an opportunity. The last one is always a quick attitude check. Even if they hate us in that moment, a grumbling spirit requires repentance. If they need to talk it out, that is always welcomed as long as they maintained the right heart while doing it. With those standards and expectations in place, they obeyed well. They were all as rambunctious as can be, but generally well behaved and very responsive whenever we needed to correct them.

Thomas had never lived in a home where decent behavior or obedience was required of him. From what I gather, he pretty much ran amok. Since the foster mother gave in to whatever he wanted just to keep him quiet, she had sabotaged herself and, therefore, my family as well. He had learned that if he stuck with it long enough, he always won. There were days I really wanted to call her up and tell her just how thankful I was for that. She had made our shopping trips so enjoyable.

It was absolute hell for us until Thomas learned that his antics were not allowed in our house, and especially not in public. I felt like all I did was punish him. It was a relentless battle of the wills, and he did his best to wear us all down. It was all I could do most days to hold everything together, and I would watch the clock for it to be time for my husband to come home from work. I'm not sure if his very presence calmed the house or if it was just me, but I was generally exhausted by dinnertime, and simply knowing I had backup made all the difference.

Daily life had become extremely busy for our family. Christopher worked two full-time jobs between ministry and what actually paid the bills. I spent my days raising the kids and maintaining the house, so my days were consumed with baseball games, school outings, never-ending piles of laundry, continuous meal prep, constant cleaning, homeschooling, and never-ending damage control. We hosted weekly Bible study groups, leadership meetings, and counseling sessions. We were regularly strategizing and planning community outreaches with our leadership team and prepping for our weekly church services.

I had a home-based business that I really enjoyed, and although I was very successful and was receiving regional recognition, something had to give. Thomas's unpredictability prevented me from being able to travel and host events. I couldn't leave him with a babysitter, and I couldn't risk taking him with me when my husband was working or had a ministry commitment. He was just too much. In the end, my business wasn't as important as my sanity, my children, or my ministry. It was a difficult sacrifice to make, and it honestly took me awhile to get over my resentment toward Thomas creating the need for me to let it go in the first place. I knew my focus had to ultimately be on him. There was really no way around it.

I had to find a way to get him to settle, but it was near impossible to find consequences that helped curb his outbursts and malicious attacks on the other children. I learned quickly that spanking him or sending him to his room was generally counterproductive. Spanking resulted in physical convulsions and screams of terror, and then he would end up feeling beaten and abused. Sending him to his room triggered all the times his foster mother kept him in his bedroom for hours on end. Sometimes I would have to send him there anyway just so everyone else could have a break, but then he would throw the furniture and kick holes in the walls and doors.

Since he showed no particular attachment to any of his belongings, removing or limiting his access to toys, television, or video games didn't garner much change in his behavior. If anything, it fostered more sneaking and more resentment toward his siblings, who continued to have the privileges that he had lost. We bribed him, guilted him, and tried reasoning with him. We punished him harshly, and we gave lots of grace. We spoke quietly to him, we yelled at him, encouraged him, and we shamed him. We tried everything, and nothing seemed to work any better or worse than any other.

I ended up making him a reward chart using stickers and magnets that hung on our refrigerator. He could lose privileges, but he could also earn them back. As rewards, we offered him candy, new toys, video games, and even money. To our surprise, those things were not enticing enough to motivate him to behave better. I continued to chart out his time-outs and groundings, however. Whatever consequences he earned, the chart helped redirect his frustration toward the chart itself instead of toward any of us.

The chart proved to be a great benefit for us, especially for me, who was the main enforcer during the daytime. The chart ensured I didn't forget to follow through with whatever consequence I gave him, and it helped me stay consistent with my words. Thomas could never seem to remember his malbehavior from one moment to the next, but the chart was there as a constant witness. When we would remind him that he couldn't play a video game because he had just hit his sister and purposely broke one of his brother's toys, he would seem confused and unable connect the two events. The chart had become our written law.

Because his consequences would usually end up compounding, I had to make it where he could see all of his consequences at once. He usually ended up being grounded for days at a time due to multiple infractions. With each new offense, something else was stripped away until there was usually nothing left. He could lose TV, video games, and playing outside all on the same day. At times, his freedom would be confined to his bedroom and his collection of books.

The chart also allowed me to keep track of what types of consequences brought out the worst reactions in him and which ones he could care less about. I learned that keeping him inside on a beautiful spring day was torture, and denying him TV access in the dead of winter was just cruel. Most punishments didn't garner much of a reaction though, but I was grasping for any clue that could help me turn the tide. I was honestly just doing my best to keep my head above water.

*****

Since most of my day was spent in the kitchen and dining area of the house, I designated the center of the kitchen as a time-out space. I placed a chair in the middle of the room where Thomas couldn't reach anything and where he had no one else to harass and nothing he could grab to throw. It took a very long time to get him to sit in the chair. Sometimes I had to literally drag him there and then chase him down as he repeatedly tried to escape.

He would do everything he could to not actually sit on the chair. He would barely rest his hip on the edge, and more often than not, he would end up falling off onto the floor. My time-outs were never very long, maybe three to five minutes at most, but I had to break his defiance and train him to obey me. So every time he fell out of the chair or tried to escape, his time would start over.

A three-minute time-out often turned into an hour, sometimes two. It was all about breaking his will and bending it toward mine. He had to sit if I told him to sit, and he had to sit correctly with his rear end fully on the seat. It went back to the all-the-way obedience and not a halfway obedience. I had to win if I ever hoped to have peace in my home again.

There were so many days I just wanted to let him go and not deal with him, but if I let myself slip and give in today, then I had an even harder battle tomorrow. He was wild and crazy, but he wasn't an idiot. Give him one inch, and he took a mile. After weeks and weeks of this, he eventually started to comply and do his time, but as soon as I would let him get up, he would go right up the stairs and hit someone—sometimes within a minute. It was like he sat there quietly only to plot his next attack.

Then I would have to go see who was crying and listen to all the upset little voices recount what had happened. Thomas would deny that it was him, of course, but I could see a smirk of satisfaction cross his face whenever he thought I wasn't looking. I would have to tell him to go back to the chair, which he would usually refuse to do. Then I would have to physically drag him to it and wrestle with him until he put his butt back on that seat again. Over and over and over, this cycle would go. Day after day. I wasn't sure it was working for the longest time, but he eventually learned that I was more determined than he was.

Consistency and staying true to our word was the only thing that created some turnaround in his behavior. The behavior chart eventually faded away. What really made the difference long-term was not wavering or giving in to him. If I told him I would spank him the next time he hit his sister, then I made sure to spank him. If he got caught hitting the neighbor boy, then he couldn't play outside for the rest of the day, period—even if he promised to not do it again and even when the neighbor boy knocked on the door and begged for me to let him come back outside.

If I tell him he won't get a Popsicle when we get home because he continually disobeyed me in the store, then I needed to make sure that the other children get one to reinforce the consequence. So many times, he would stand there waiting for his turn, and then he would be so disappointed when I would shut the freezer door. I would have to ignore my desire to give in and give him one too. His genuine disappointment was heartbreaking, but he had to be taught that life was made up of choices, good and bad, and we all reap from the choices that we make.

I would constantly have to repeat to him the decisions he had made and the consequence it had created. I would have to remind him that if he wanted that reward tomorrow, then he better listen and obey me today. Grace was given, but it was given sparingly because grace wasn't helpful. Grace wasn't seen as a merciful, loving act but as a time he got away with something. It was constant daily conditioning and training that was emotionally exhausting. At least each day provided our other three children ample opportunities to practice forgiveness.

CHAPTER 7

The Lord is merciful and gracious,
slow to anger and abounding in steadfast love.
—Psalm 103:8

I had hoped that the outburst I endured in the airport on the day I brought him home was a onetime event caused by all of the uncertainty and circumstances of the day, but it didn't take long before those were happening regularly in our home. Thomas came to us with a deep, deep well of rage, and that rage would explode with little to no warning.

The more we fought to gain control over him and his behaviors, the worse it got. He would scream at the top of his lungs, turning his face deep red while his whole body would shake, and his fists would clinch, ready to strike. He would get himself so worked up that he would burst some of his blood vessels and bleed from his ears and nose. It was as if a beast took over his body. It would escalate to such a dangerous level that he was a threat to himself and to everyone else around him. He would swing his fists and kick his legs so wildly that anything in his path was beaten or smashed to pieces. His anger was intense, and very tangible.

We tried to figure out what it was that would trigger such outbursts, but there never seemed to be anything specific. It could be anything that made him angry or something you were trying to make him do that he just didn't want to do. One particular time, I asked him to put on his shoes after church so we could go to lunch. He preferred to do things on his own as much as possible, so I had him sit down, and I handed him his shoes. This time, though, he didn't want to put them on. I tried to explain to him that it was time to go and that everyone else was leaving too, thinking maybe he wanted to stay and keep playing.

When I took the shoes back and began to put them on him myself, he kicked his feet and started pushing on me. So I gave him his shoes again and told him that either he put them on himself, or I was going to have to do it for him. He had to make a choice. He just sat there as the lights were being turned off and everyone else was heading for the door. After a few minutes of silence and him refusing to do anything, I once again explained that refusing to choose was also a choice. Not choosing meant that I would have to do it for him.

Of course, he started fighting against me when I tried to put them on his feet again. I could sense that he was on the verge of exploding, so I got his father's attention and asked him to step in and help. It took both of us, but his shoes ended up on his feet. Then he refused to stand up or walk. His legs went limp when we stood him up. Once again, I gave him a choice. Either he was going to walk on his own, or we were going to have to carry him.

Choice usually got him to cooperate because it gave him some sense of control over his life, and it encouraged him to obey and do what we asked of him. We were pretty much guaranteed a battle whenever he didn't like either of the choices we offered. His legs remained limp, and he refused to look at us, answer us, or stand up. Christopher scooped him up and started carrying him to the door.

You would have thought that he was being abused in some way. He went from a stoic and silent defiance to screaming and flailing wildly. It turned into a wrestling match exactly like the one we witnessed out front of the foster home and the one I encountered at the airport. He was kicking and pushing, pounding his fists against his father's body, and wiggling himself to try to release his grip. My husband had gotten used to physically restraining him, so he expected the struggle and tightened his grip all the more.

Christopher carried him down the aisle, out the front entrance, and all the way to our van, where he was finally released. Thomas was so out of control that it wasn't safe for us to get into the vehicle with him. We had learned to lock him in and let him rage it out where he could be contained. We stood in the parking lot while everyone else pulled away, waiting for it to be safe enough to get in and leave ourselves.

There is no other way to describe Thomas's appearance other than to say he embodied rage itself. His whole face contorted. He was screaming and cursing at us so violently that his veins popped out of his neck and spit was flying from his mouth. He spewed every vile curse he could think of in our direction. He started hitting the glass windows and grabbing at the seats, trying to tear the fabric. He even tried to pick them up to throw them through the windows, but of course, his little frame wasn't strong enough to make them budge.

This wasn't the first time we had to wrestle him out of a building and into a vehicle. It happened more times than I can count. We learned that the only thing we could do was to turn our backs to him and deny him an audience. He would eventually exhaust himself and calm down, but sometimes we would have to stand there for half an hour until it was safe enough to get in and drive home. We did everything we could to not have to take him into public places because we never knew when he would explode.

It would have been very helpful to have a containment room or a basement space available in our home. Instead, we would have to hold him from behind or wrestle him down to the floor and pin him where he couldn't move. We would hold his arms down with our hands and use our body weight to pin his legs to the floor. He would fight against us and try to knock us off him. His rage made him surprisingly strong. When he couldn't get his arms and legs free, he would gnash his teeth and try to bite our wrists. He would use his fingers to scratch at them to try to make us let him go.

He would scream profanities at us and tell us how much he hated us while blood would be pouring down his face and down the sides of his neck. We would speak to him very calmly the whole time and try to get him to gain control of himself, but it always took time. Whichever one of us that would have to end up restraining him would be covered in sweat and exhausted, but he would eventually give in and relax enough for us to let him go. We would then speak to him about whatever it was that had set him off, clean him up, and continue about our day.

We dealt with these rage fits for the first two or three years until they gradually decreased in frequency and severity. He eventually learned how to suppress it. He continued to get angry with us, of course—that will never change—but he would resort more to throwing things, slamming doors, and yelling at us to make sure we knew just how unfair we were being toward him. He would never speak of his inner rage with us or with a therapist. It has become a permanent part of who he is, and it is always simmering just under the surface of his control.

Although all of our efforts eventually modified Thomas's outward behavior, it didn't affect his inward mind-set. He just learned to hide what he was doing and to be craftier with his approach. His jealousy and resentment toward the other children was still present. His anger toward us as parental figures remained. His insecurities and fears have never left him. His identity as the abandoned, unlovable adopted child has always shaped who he views himself to be. No matter how many times we have told him that he is loved and that he was chosen to be a part of our family, he will not—cannot—believe us.

*****

Much of our struggles with Thomas have been due to reactive attachment disorder or RAD. It is imperative to understand RAD to understand Thomas and other children like him. As the years have passed, we have gained a greater understanding of how this disorder has shaped who he is and our relationship with him. He was diagnosed with RAD at the age of two. That is extremely early for any kind of mental health or behavioral diagnosis.

His caseworker told us that he was diagnosed with RAD as we were initiating the adoption process, but we wanted to give Thomas a fresh start without all the labels and biases that were placed on him at such a young age. That was mostly due to the cruel way his foster mother spoke about him, and the alarming way his therapist reacted to him. We wanted a clean slate for him, and we wanted to give time for him to adjust to his new family, his new identity, and to give way to a season of healing. We had hoped that some behaviors would work themselves out with time and stability.

We didn't fully understand a lot about reactive attachment at first, and it wasn't until he was around ten years old that RAD was listed as an official diagnosis for him again. Doctors will testify that the first five years of a child's life is crucial to their growth and development, especially on their mental well-being. Research states that in the first thirty-six months of life alone, a child's brain grows to 90 percent of its adult size. In recent years, scientists have begun studying the effects of abandonment, abuse, neglect, and even violence on the developing brains of children under the age of five.

Brain scans have shown that children who have experienced significant trauma in their formative years have smaller brains than those who haven't experienced trauma. Their brain development appears to be stunted. Atrophy is suspected to be a major contributor to cognitive delays, behavioral problems, and mental health issues, including severe depression. It is believed that once the brain growth is stunted, there is no way to ever reverse the damage. In some of these cases, researchers have actually found holes in the brains of children. These holes are suspected to interfere with the brain's ability to think consequentially.

I have read research that suggests that in addition to the size and development of the brain tissue, the chemical distribution within the brain is also interrupted. There is a decrease of the corpus callosum that connects the right side with the left side of the brain. The corpus callosum controls the neurotransmitters that affect a child's mood, behavior, and overall function. These neurotransmitters control the chemicals that excite and calm the brain. They are developed over time as the child is shown love, security, and as his basic needs are met. When notable neglect or trauma is experienced before these transmitters are fully developed, the result is a chemical imbalance that creates a hypervigilant state of fear and stress.

I do not pretend to understand the brain and all of its functions. I am not a neurologist, but I have done my best to understand the physical ramifications of trauma and abuse on the brain's development and what that means in regard to RAD. The research you can access on the topic can be overwhelming and also very discouraging. These children seem to remain mentally impaired and chemically imbalanced for the rest of their lives. They are unable to develop the ability to fully bond and form healthy attachments to other individuals. When doctors recognize these conditions in a child, it leads them to a reactive attachment diagnosis.

RAD was officially recognized as a mental health disorder after studying children who had been placed in orphanages. The study was conducted specifically on the lasting effects of institutional care. RAD was added to the American Psychiatric Association's third edition of *Diagnostic and Statistical Manual of Mental Disorders* in 1980. That is a very recent addition for mental health. Everything I have studied suggests that there is still a great need for more understanding and research to be done on children who have been in the foster care system, specifically those who have been adopted out of it.

Many mental health professionals remain undereducated about RAD, and there has been much debate surrounding the cause and treatment of the condition. The few treatments that are being used are controversial in regard to their overall effectiveness. Mental health professionals rely on medications to help modify behaviors and to stabilize the mood and chemical distributions within these children's brains. Some say ongoing treatment can cure RAD while others say there is little that can be done. There is no known cure for reactive attachment disorder.

According to the latest statistics released from the US Department of Health and Human Services' AFCARS Report, there were 437,465 children in foster care in 2016 with 117,794 children waiting to be adopted. These numbers are slowly increasing year after year. The highest percentage of children being placed in the foster care system is before the age of one with 95 percent being due to neglect and parental drug abuse. The average amount of time a child spends in foster care is about nineteen months while those children waiting to be adopted are in care closer to thirty-one months.

This report tells us that the average child who has been placed in foster care is not reunited with a family member until they are about three years old. If parental rights are severed and the child becomes eligible for adoption, they are statistically between the ages of four and five when they are placed in adoptive homes, as was our experience. These statistics are, of course, averages. Thousands are placed quickly while thousands more wait indefinitely.

These children have experienced major disruption and instability during their most formidable months of life, hindering their ability to bond and form healthy attachments that are crucial for proper brain development. Upward of 80 percent of all children in the foster care system have been diagnosed with significant mental health issues compared to only about 20 percent of the general population.

RAD behaviors have also been identified in children who grow up with their biological parents, but without intervention, they may not recognize the effects that parental drug abuse, neglect, or sexual and physical abuse has had on them until well into adulthood, if at all. There is no way to track the effects of RAD in those situations. Once a RAD child reaches adulthood, their mental health issues are categorized as a personality disorder or a mood disorder, which is why we don't hear of adults being diagnosed with reactive attachment.

I believe reactive attachment is a self-perpetuating disorder. RAD children enter adulthood with significant cognitive impairment and mental health issues. They lack the ability to maintain long-term, healthy relationships, and if they have children of their own, they have difficulty caring and bonding with them. Statistically, teens and adults who have mental health issues tend to self-medicate with drugs and alcohol, which can lead to neglectful, erratic, and sometimes abusive behaviors. If these behaviors have created an unstable or unhealthy situation for their own children and have hindered proper bonding in any way, then they have inadvertently perpetuated the RAD cycle.

Researchers have identified two types of reactive attachment: inhibited and disinhibited. Children diagnosed with RAD usually fall under one of these types, but they can exhibit both types of behaviors at different times in their development. Disinhibited RAD is where the child seeks inappropriate attention from anyone without discrimination. They frequently ask for help, and they can become inappropriately familiar with other people. They can display childish behaviors, and they can regularly violate socially acceptable boundaries. Inhibited RAD is where the child is withdrawn and detached from others. They avoid and shun relationships and are unresponsive to being physically comforted.

To understand RAD is to understand Thomas. When we began to research RAD more thoroughly and I found a checklist of possible behaviors, Thomas exhibited every single behavior except cruelty to animals. His foster mother claimed that he had harmed her animals, but we have never witnessed that. We have consistently had pets in our home, and he has always been very tender and loving toward them. Other than cruelty to animals, he is basically a textbook case, which is what probably led to his very early diagnosis. To fully understand what I mean, I have summarized RAD behaviors into the following six categories.

Developmental Delays and Social Behaviors

Children with RAD are usually developmentally and socially delayed where they can display abnormal and odd behaviors. Thomas has many behaviors that would be considered abnormal and fit within a RAD diagnosis. He dresses differently than his peers and doesn't bathe with regularity, hardly brushes his hair, and almost never brushes his teeth. He fidgets and has nonsensical movements and regularly paces back and forth and openly and obsessively chews on things.

RAD children tend to have comprehension and speech delays, which Thomas exhibited very young. He has remained slow to speak and is known to talk in circles or give answers that do not make any sense at all. He is often mentally clouded and is emotionally immature with a strange and immature sense of humor, which falls within RAD behavioral markers. Unfortunately, as he has gotten older, other children have been known to make fun of him or avoid him altogether.

RAD children tend to be impulsive, have abnormal eating habits, and tend to have toilet issues. Thomas has always had weird eating habits from the things he would or would not eat to how often he would eat. He also lacks the impulse control of how much he can eat at one time, resulting in binge eating at odd times of the day. As far as his bathroom behaviors, Thomas wet himself regularly as a child, but he could also hold his urine for excessive amounts of time. Whenever he finally decided to go, he would spend extended periods of time doing so.

Unpredictability and Violence

Children with RAD can have severe mood swings and unpredictable behaviors. The simplest of things would trigger violent outbursts for Thomas, and he can switch from one emotion to another within minutes. We spent a lot of energy assessing his mood and carefully interacting with him in effort to avoid any negative reactions or sudden outbursts. As he reached adolescence, his moods became darker, more severe, and more violent. He entertains fantasies of wanting to harm others and to enact revenge on those who he feels have mistreated or harmed him in any way.

Unhealthy Attachments

RAD children do not understand what a healthy emotional attachment is because they were not able to form proper attachments in their earlier stages of development. If someone notices the neglect, then they are often shuffled through multiple placements within the foster care system, which can be very traumatic and lead to heightened levels of stress, insecurity, and fear.

Research has shown that RAD children subsequently form unhealthy bonds with adults and peers throughout their lifetime. When Thomas was little, he would wander off from us and follow strangers, usually adult men. He had a hard time recognizing who was his family and who was not, who was safe and who was a stranger. He wouldn't allow us to hold his hand, so we would have to chase him down and bring him back to us over and over again.

Thomas would crawl up into the laps of visitors he didn't know, and he would smile and act very charming toward them. On the surface, he would seem to be bonding with them. Many people have been fooled by this type of behavior, including our extended family and friends. They would have no way of knowing that moments before their arrival, he was screaming and terrorizing everyone else in the house; but as soon as they had arrived, he became the sweet, innocent little boy who was the victim of everyone else around him.

In general, RAD children are great manipulators. They learn how to put on the charm to get what they want. They spin their reality by the truths that they create in their own minds, and they are known to tell tales that you would not think to question. This is actually a great survival technique to get their needs met when they would otherwise go without. Over the years, we have seen this manipulative behavior fool many people, including his therapists, caseworkers, and even police officers.

Thomas has never bonded with our family, and we know now that he most likely never will. He is just not capable. As humans, we are created to bond with others; but when that capability doesn't develop for us in infancy, we are left in a constant state of push and pull. RAD children know that there should be an attachment. There is an innate need to attach, but there is an inability to make it happen. They push others away but then resent those they push away for not being there and not being connected to them.

Those with reactive attachment can be envious or even resentful of attachments they see between other people. Within a bonded family unit, the incoming foster or adopted RAD child can take their own lack of attachment and place those feelings on the other family members where they feel personally rejected. Then in effort to protect themselves from that perceived rejection, they in turn reject, which inadvertently perpetuates the very cycle that makes them feel isolated and alone in the first place.

With RAD children not being able to trust and feel connected to the people around them, they tend to develop shallow and dysfunctional relationships based on their own perception of reality. Thomas has always been drawn to other children that are socially awkward, developmentally delayed, rebellious, mentally ill, or those that display violent tendencies. His relationships with them are usually mutually manipulative and destructive. These friends use him as much as he uses them, and they tend to feed off one another and get in a lot of trouble.

Destructive Behaviors

RAD children tend to be very destructive to themselves and to those around them. They can display risky behaviors without concern for their own well-being or the well-being of others. They also do not value their own belongings or the belongings of others. Thomas has destroyed everything we have ever given him, sometimes within the same day. If you would compare his room with the rooms of his siblings, their toy bins would be overflowing while his would be sparse and contain only broken remnants of what he once had.

When we have purchased expensive electronic devices such as phones or tablets for him, it was just a matter of time before they were broken, disassembled, or missing. He would then complain that he didn't have a device like his siblings. When we would ask him where his went, he would just say that he didn't know. If we refused to purchase him another one, he would get angry and usually seek out someone else's device to steal or destroy in an act of revenge and jealousy.

RAD children tend to be fire starters, and with all the times he has been angry with us, I have wondered if he would try to burn our house down. For many years, we didn't own any lighters or matches, but somehow he always found some and brought them home. I would find burnt papers, cotton swabs, and even singed pencils in his bed where he would play with fire during the night. I have offered many prayers of thanksgiving for the fact that he hasn't caught himself or his bed on fire.

One day, he decided to roll up some school papers on the bus and light them on fire so it would look like he was smoking a large blunt. He didn't think through that it would create a lot of smoke and be potentially dangerous if he lost control of the flame. The bus driver immediately turned the bus around, and Thomas was removed from the bus by the principal. Of course, he denied it, even after the other children quickly admitted it was he who had started the fire and that he had thrown the papers out the window as the bus was being turned around.

Thomas was convinced he was being targeted by the principal and mistreated by the bus driver because RAD children do not understand cause and effect. He can never comprehend why someone would be upset with him or how any of his actions would result in him being punished. He was suspended from the bus for the remainder of the school year, but he never wavered in his innocence. He remains convinced that he was unfairly treated to this day.

Lack of Morality

RAD children are said to not be capable of feeling guilt or showing remorse for their behaviors. We have noticed that Thomas has never been able to empathize with others. He does not understand that he can be the cause of someone else's pain or that he can cause others to experience loss. If he breaks something irreplaceable or hurts your feelings with his harsh words, he is completely unaware of how that might make you feel.

Statistically, RAD children do not understand faith or religion. They cannot comprehend believing in something or someone they cannot see. RAD children can lack a moral compass and, therefore, not comprehend why something would be considered wrong to do. They also tend to act out sexually and are usually addicted to pornography. We have found horrific forms of pornography on our computers involving violent rape and incest. We have had to invest in protection programs and change our passwords regularly to hinder his ability to access inappropriate things online.

Reactive-attachment children are also known to be nonsensical liars, and they can steal without any remorse or fear of being caught. They are incapable of taking ownership of their actions. Thomas is a master thief who has been repeatedly caught with stolen items in his possession, which he adamantly denies to be his doing. If you press him enough about a stolen or missing item or asked him the same question in different ways, he usually ends up admitting and denying everything he has done within the same conversation.

Defiance of Authority

RAD children typically trust no one. They are very defiant of authority and rely only on themselves. They are compelled to defy, even when you can tell that they don't necessarily want to. It is ingrained in them to resist, to disobey, and to mistrust. Experience has taught them that adults fail you. They neglect you, abandon you, and control you. Thomas will refuse any kind of advice or help from an adult simply because it has come from an adult.

When Thomas expressed a desire to be a zookeeper when he grew up, I researched a summer program that he could join where he could volunteer at our local zoo. As soon as we responded positively to his interest, he immediately rejected it. Being a zookeeper was now "stupid." The next time he expressed an interest, we made sure to remain more neutral, but then he became angry with us for not cheering him on and took our reserved reaction as disapproval and rejection. Either way, we could never win.

RAD children are also known to give false accusations of physical or sexual abuse. We have had many investigators in our home over the years interrogating our other three children because of things that Thomas has said that have put us under suspicion. Most of his accusations have been directed toward me specifically, more than any other member of the family. His accusations have ruined relationships with neighbors. Whenever we have noticed that they have started avoiding eye contact with us and have clearly forbidden their children from playing with ours, we know to suspect that it is probably because of something Thomas has told them.

RAD children usually struggle with the idea that someone would dare to love them. For Thomas, this feeling has filtered everything through a perception that we are perpetually opposed to him and that we actually hate him. Hand in hand with that, RAD children tend to have very low self-esteem. Deep down, they are very depressed. They can have overwhelming feelings of sadness and hopelessness.

Most RAD children struggle in school and tend to drop out. Once they reach adulthood, they can have difficulty keeping employment due to their defiance to authority, so they often find themselves homeless. They can continue to struggle to form real, healthy, lasting relationships with other people throughout their lifetime. Many of them find themselves in legal trouble due to their aggression and anger toward everyone else around them.

CHAPTER 8

The Lord is close to the brokenhearted
and saves those who are crushed in spirit.
—Psalm 34:18

I never wanted to be one of those "homeschooling moms." The homeschooling families I knew were very nice but a little quirky. I was afraid that homeschooling my children would make them weird. I fully intended on sending my children through regular school, but our oldest son, Jacob, is autistic; and by the time he was in the first grade, he had academically surpassed his classmates. His idea of fun was doing advanced algebra.

Jacob started coming home from school and telling us that his teacher had gotten frustrated with him again and had made him put his head down on his desk. She had started forbidding him from participating in class because he wanted to learn things like greater than and less than instead of his ABCs. He was already reading at a fourth-grade level. He couldn't understand why he was being punished for asking to learn more advanced material. I could see that he was starting to dislike school.

When Christopher and I spoke to his teacher about it, she admitted that she didn't like that he knew all the answers and that he kept asking her to teach him different things. She confirmed that he was being told to put his head down on his desk. Of course, we went straight to the administration. After getting him evaluated, it was determined that although he was advanced academically, he was much smaller than his peers, and he was not socially mature enough to move up to a high enough grade level where he would be challenged academically. After a couple of months, everyone involved determined that schooling him at home would be his best option.

By the time Thomas came to live with us, I had been home-schooling for four years, and it was working well for our family. The adoptive state made us agree that we would never homeschool Thomas. We have every legal right to make educational decisions for our other children, but for that first year, Thomas didn't technically belong to us. We were only his foster parents. Right away, Thomas asked to stay home and do school along with everyone else. He didn't like getting up early and having to go to preschool when he knew everyone else was still home in their pajamas, especially through the cold winter months.

After a year, we were told that we could begin the process of finalizing our adoption. We arranged with the court to have his adoption day fall on his sixth birthday. Following our court hearing, we went to an indoor play place and threw him a huge party with all of our friends and family. It was an amazing day of celebration. The following morning, we went straight to his school and withdrew him. The state wasn't pleased with us, but there wasn't anything they could say now that he was legally ours and under our custody.

Homeschooling Thomas didn't last for very long. I hung in there with him through first and second grade. Some days were manageable, and a little bit of progress would be made, but other days just turned into a battle of the wills like everything else. After the first year, I swore I would never homeschool him again, but there were so many layers and layers of emotional and behavioral issues we were working through that I decided to give him one more year. I knew he wouldn't get the individual attention in public school that he needed. Homeschooling him also seemed to be the best way to solidify his place within the family without him feeling separated and different from the rest of the children.

It didn't take long for Thomas to learn our daily routine, but getting him to sit down and focus on something for any amount of time was a challenge. Some days he would sit through his lessons really well and complete all of his assignments, but there were other days that he just didn't want to work. On those days, he would usually pick a fight with someone so that he would be sent out of the room. When Thomas decided to work, he worked slowly. When his siblings would finish for the day, he would become very agitated, especially on days where he was the last one still working.

Our biggest struggle happened whenever I would ask Thomas to write his name on his paper or to write down his answer to a question. He would usually refuse to pick up his pencil. Fifteen minutes could go by before he would put it in his hand, and even then, he would barely hold it. He would keep his hand limp and flop the pencil across his paper, not making any marks at all. He moved his hand as if it was full of Jell-O, and he had no control over what he was doing. When I would insist that he comply, he would just sit there with a blank expression on his face and not utter a word. If I put the pencil in his hand myself, he would let it roll away as if he was unable to grasp it.

We could be having a great discussion about a lesson, and he could be answering all the questions correctly, but when I would ask him to pick up his pencil, he would regularly refuse. It wasn't because he didn't know how to write his name on his paper or that he didn't know the answer to one of the questions. He just didn't want to comply. It was so infuriating and a constant struggle to know when to push him and when to just send him away and be done for the day. I could yell at him and ask him why he was refusing with absolutely no response. I could wait him out and leave him sitting silently for an hour or more, and he would still refuse. At that point, he was only punishing himself because the other children would be playing outside or even eating lunch, but there would sit Thomas in silent defiance.

I think that his refusal to comply was mostly due to the fact that his foster mother had bred a rebellion and a defiance within him that became ingrained in the very fabric of who he is. There is something in him that absolutely prevents him from obeying whatever it is you have told him to do. It could be anything. It could be something that directly benefits him and him alone, but because it requires him to do what you say, he still won't do it.

One day, ice cream came up. I'm not sure who suggested it—probably me. So I told everyone to get their shoes on, and we would take a drive over to the ice-cream shop and have an afternoon treat. The other kids were out the door in a flash, but there stood Thomas, looking at his shoes. When I asked him if he wanted to go get ice cream, he shook his head yes. I could tell he sincerely wanted to. So I waited. He usually moved at a snail's pace, so I had learned to be patient; most of the time I was successful. He was often so slow that you could barely see him moving at all, but if you said anything to him or directly told him to hurry up, he slowed down even more or came to a complete halt.

If you jumped in to help him, he would get upset with you because he was already doing it. So you would have to wait even longer for him to get over the intrusion, focus on the task again, and then muster up enough gumption to continue. So here I was waiting in silence for him to do something. After a few minutes, he was still standing there, obviously having an internal struggle. The other kids had already buckled themselves in and shut the car doors. I asked him again if he was sure he wanted ice cream, and he again shook his head yes. I asked him what the problem was then, and he shrugged his shoulders and said he couldn't put his shoes on. When I asked him why, he said he just couldn't because I had told him to.

Whenever we have discussed our struggles with other people, we have often been told that ODD or oppositional defiance disorder isn't a real thing and that it is simply rebellion. If you have ever dealt with ODD, it is far worse than what people view as your typical adolescent rebellion. I have been lectured on how I just need to have clear-cut boundaries and strict consequences put in place for him whenever he refuses to obey. If I would just be consistent with him, he would learn that I mean business, and he would simply fall in line. That may be true for many children, but that is not oppositional defiance disorder. I actually wish it was that easy! It definitely helps to be strict and consistent, but that doesn't make the behaviors or the thought patterns go away.

In some of our more difficult times, well-meaning people have gifted my husband and me with parenting books. Giving us books on teenage rebellion with steps on how to discipline your wild child means that they're not really listening to what we are saying. It is hard enough to navigate through all of the challenges this disorder brings without also feeling like we need to defend ourselves or our experiences with the people around us. I have been argued with so many times on whether or not ODD is a legitimate thing that I just don't discuss it with anyone anymore.

Those parenting books sit dusty on my bookshelf to this day. Neither one of us read them because they simply do not apply to our situation. They are probably very good books, but Christopher and I don't need parenting advice on discipline. We've taught numerous parenting classes ourselves and have helped many young families with parenting issues over the years. Putting boundaries and consequences in place have never been a stumbling block for either one of us. If anything, we've been too strict. We are some of the most consistent parents you will ever meet, and our older three children are a testament to that fact.

Oppositional defiance goes much deeper than your standard variety of rebellious behaviors. ODD is classified as a personality disorder. A personality disorder is only able to be diagnosed if there are clear impairments with the way a person interacts with others around them. This would include how that person feels emotion and then what they do with that emotion.

You have to take what is considered socially normal and then compare that with the way a person with ODD interprets situations and how they think about problems. These differences have to be consistent over long periods of time and remain the same through multiple situations because a personality disorder doesn't change depending upon a particular situation or a major life event.

Personality disorders develop early on in life and never change. It isn't age related. They don't grow out of it. It isn't something that can be changed by simply creating rules and boundaries. It is associated with a significant disability that displays maladaptive coping skills, combined with a very deep depression. Because of that, ODD teens are prone to self-medicate and abuse drugs to cope with their mental state, which is often misconstrued by outsiders as simple rebellious behavior that can be easily corrected with proper parenting.

Oppositional defiance disorder is not related to a teenager who has never been taught to respect adults or who wants to simply buck authority. It is not about expressing their angst against their parent, partying and wanting to just have fun, or acting out while trying to cope with a particularly difficult situation in their family or personal life. It goes much deeper than that.

So that you can better understand, here are the three different types of personality disorders: type A, B, and C. Unfortunately, Thomas displays some characteristics from all three. Type A is classified as having odd, eccentric, and bizarre behavior. A person with this type of personality disorder has a pattern of paranoia, irrational suspicion, and overall mistrust of other people. They are always on the lookout for clues to validate their suspicions.

They are overly sensitive to personal failure, criticism, and any type of real or perceived rejection. Once an offense has been determined by them, they hold strong grudges that can last throughout their whole lifetime. They tend to have a distorted perception of reality and interpret other people's actions as malicious. They are uncomfortable and disinterested in social interactions and spend a lot of time alone. They usually show very little emotion, and they can be detached and aloof with other people.

Type B is characterized by extreme mood swings. Individuals with this type of ODD tend to be irritable, aggressive, and impulsive. They can appear to be charming, but they lack empathy and have a disregard for the personal rights of others. They don't understand why someone would be angry with them, and they do not learn from their mistakes.

Sometimes their personality disorder manifests as an attention-seeking behavior with erratic or dramatic emotional outbursts that sometimes involve self-harm. They usually have a skewed self-image so they have a need to be admired. This personality type can be very manipulative, so they often have unstable relationships with others. This type is most associated with crime, and they tend to be in and out of prison throughout their lifetime.

Type C personality disorder is characterized by fear and anxiety. People with this type feel socially inadequate. They have a fear of being embarrassed, criticized, or rejected. They withdraw from social situations and can avoid meeting new people unless they are sure they will be liked and approved of. They are very aware of the reactions of others and are very introspective. They tend to depend on other people to take care of them because they can have difficulty making everyday decisions. They can be very particular and controlling of their environment and have obsessive-compulsive behaviors that take precedence over anything else, especially relationships.

Some RAD and ODD behaviors are similar to each other and overlap. With Thomas, it can be difficult for me to distinguish what is reactive attachment and what is oppositional defiance. Together they have shaped how Thomas behaves, how he feels about the world around him, and how he interacts with me and the rest of the family. When you remove the bonding aspect of RAD, he seems to be less agitated and has a greater freedom to interact with other people on a superficial level. Maybe it is because they don't have to matter to him, and he can simply walk away whenever he feels like it and remain completely detached. He is not expected to fully engage with people outside of the immediate family.

I understand that many children are diagnosed as having ODD and other behavioral problems when they probably don't have them at all. I believe we can be too quick to label children with disorders and medicate them in our society. Sometimes it is a parenting issue and a disruptive homelife that needs to be corrected. That is why understanding the specifics about each diagnosis is important so that a true understanding can be obtained. I think there needs to be caution given when speaking to another parent about their child's struggles, even if you are family. Unless you live in the home, there are dynamics at work that you may never be able to fully understand. My advice is to please listen and try to understand before dismissing someone else's struggle, no matter the context.

*****

Thomas went back to public school in the third grade. Because of his RAD and ODD, he was unable to learn or take any real instruction from me. It was also a benefit to everyone else in the home to have time during the day without him around. We didn't hear of him having any major issues at school in the third grade, but two months into his fourth grade year, his teacher contacted us.

Up until this point, Thomas was not on any medications and hadn't been seeing a therapist. The therapist that we were referred to after he came to live with us said that he was doing well, that he seemed to be acclimating with the family, all things considered, and that we were managing his behaviors appropriately. He dismissed us as clients when Thomas was only five years old.

We were new to the whole therapy process and didn't know what to expect. We were just trying to navigate everything one day at a time, and since the therapist said we were doing well, we trusted it. We knew we were at least giving it our best effort, and Thomas was still quite young. Without his full participation and ability to verbalize what he was feeling, my husband and I didn't see how the therapy sessions were making a real difference for him. The therapist seemed to be more focused on the adoption aspect and the general blending of him into our family than on anything else.

I wonder now if that therapist understood RAD. We never really discussed it in any of our sessions other than the fact that it was listed as a diagnosis. Maybe he didn't know what to do therapeutically to help him. We were just learning what RAD was ourselves, so we didn't know how to advocate for our family in that regard. In our final session, the therapist warned us that there was usually an uptick of problems with any kind of mental illness around puberty and to come back then if we needed to.

By the time Thomas was in the fourth grade, we had managed to contain most of his destructiveness—at least to a manageable level. Things had leveled out, and our homelife was fairly normal and routine. We didn't have to physically restrain him anymore, and he had acclimated as best as he could to the family. We still had daily challenges, of course, but we were surviving, and we were hopeful that he would continue to improve even more as he grew.

When Thomas's teacher asked us to come to the school to meet with her, she said that she had noticed a change in him. At home, we hadn't noticed anything, but she said he had stopped participating in class and had pretty much stopped doing his assignments. She said that at the beginning of the school year, he had been enthusiastic when he saw her because he really liked her, but as the weeks went by, she said he wasn't even reacting when she spoke to him anymore.

She suggested that he start seeing the school's psychologist that comes to the school twice a week. She said he seemed to be very sad, and she was concerned that Thomas was dealing with depression. We were able to get his therapy sessions scheduled right away, and Thomas was able to leave his classroom during the school day for his appointments.

We really liked the new psychologist. She was a little eccentric, but she was like your favorite crazy aunt that you could just sit and talk to for hours. She was very unassuming and would put you at ease in a moment. She was exactly what Thomas needed. It didn't take long for him to open up to her, and she would regularly catch us right after school to fill us in on their conversations. For the very first time, we were getting insight into who Thomas was and how he thinks.

He has never spoken to any of us about anything personal. If someone would have asked me his favorite color, I could guess that it was green, but I really wasn't sure. During checkups, doctors have asked how he was doing in school or with his peers, but I didn't really have anything to share. We didn't know that much about who he was. He would never think to tell us how he was feeling or what he liked or disliked, even when we asked him. He had remained an enigma after all these years.

We could rarely tell if he was happy or sad or anything. The only consistent emotion we ever saw was anger, and even then, he was really unable to express what had made him so angry. We would attempt to speak to him, but he would usually just sit there, maybe shrug his shoulders. Sometimes one single tear would fall down his cheek. No matter what, he always kept his mouth shut.

Thankfully, the therapist figured out that if she kept his hands moving, his mouth would also move, so she got him crocheting and stitching hand puppets. I think because she wasn't a parental figure or held any kind of authoritative role in his life, he felt safe enough to open up and share with her some of his struggles. I so desperately wanted him to be able to do that with me, or anyone else in the family for that matter. If he could just learn to trust us enough to be open with us, so much of his inward struggle and rage would be relieved.

Opening up to her just proved to me that he was capable. He just didn't want to open up to any of us. Realizing that made the chasm between him and me seem even wider. It was another example of his rejection toward me specifically. I hated that he felt so isolated and alone in the world. I had tried every kind of bonding technique that I knew of, but I only reminded him of the foster mother who was cruel, his therapist who was always analyzing him, and the social worker who kept him away from his birth mother. I specifically paid the price for them and for the shortcomings of his biological parents.

It didn't take long before the psychologist became very concerned. She slyly started evaluating and testing his mental state without him knowing what she was doing. She reviewed his history and his past diagnoses. She confirmed his reactive attachment disorder (RAD), his oppositional defiance disorder (ODD), and she recognized that he had post-traumatic stress disorder (PTSD) from the abuse and that he was very clinically depressed. She referred him to a psychiatrist so that he could start on medication right away to balance out his mood and improve his overall ability to cope.

During one session, he started sharing with her how he hears voices speaking to him. He said that he hears a woman's voice that tells him that he is stupid and unlovable. He hears a young male voice that tells him to run away, and he hears an older male voice that tells him that he should just kill himself because nobody wants him around. We suspect that these voices represent his foster mother, foster father, and the foster boy who lived in the same home with him. We will never know for sure, but it could possibly explain their correlation to some prevalent trauma in his life.

Thomas then expressed to her how he felt that the world was against him. This is when paranoid schizophrenia was added to the conversation. You don't typically diagnose someone so young with such a serious prognosis, but that was taken into account as the doctors were determining which type of medications to give him. The goal was to get the voices to go away more than whether or not that needed to be added to his ever growing list of conditions.

After a few weeks, it was still difficult to judge how well the medications were improving his mental state because he never opened up to us, even as his overall mood lifted. Any questions we asked, he avoided answering. We also had to be careful not to betray the trust that he had built with his therapist because he didn't know that she was reporting back to us what he was sharing with her. He continued to see her weekly through his fourth and fifth grade years, even through the summer months.

He was able to engage with his teachers a little more and marginally improved in school. With his RAD and cognitive delays, along with his inability to think rationally and consequentially, school had become a challenge for him. We could tell that he was getting confused by the lessons and that he was completing his worksheets with answers that didn't make any sense. He was falling more and more behind his classmates.

CHAPTER 9

I called to the Lord in my distress,
and I cried to my God for help.
From his temple he heard my voice.
—Psalm 18:6

By the end of Thomas's fifth grade year, our family entered a season of great change. My husband and I had resigned our pastorate, transitioned ourselves out of the church we had founded, and began making preparations to move out of state to become full-time missionaries. Once we had a moving date, we spoke to Thomas's doctors about the relocation and how it would affect his med management. We made sure to see his psychiatrist right before we left so that we could leave with a three-month supply of medication, which is the maximum of what they could legally prescribe at one time.

The medications he was taking were very strong narcotics. They are federally regulated, and since they specifically target the brain's chemistry, they can be harmful to your mental stability if you do not take them consistently. They were not something we wanted to suddenly run out of. His medications were the only thing that seemed to be helping him cope with daily life and keeping his mood stable. I was hopeful that three months would provide us with enough time to relocate, get settled in, and find him a new psychiatrist.

Two days after we arrived and got everything moved into our new home, I began the process of getting Thomas's insurance situation changed over to our new state. As part of our adoption agreement, all of Thomas's medical expenses are covered by his birth state until he turns eighteen years old. Since we changed states, we had to initiate an Interstate Compact on Adoption Medical Assistance

(ICAMA). This agreement between our state and the adoptive state was taken care of through our adoption process, and we didn't have to be involved the first time around. This time, I didn't even know what the professional term was that I needed. I just knew that I had to initiate a new agreement between my new state and the state where Thomas was born.

I quickly discovered that there was no place to physically go where I could speak to an actual human being face-to-face. Everything related to social services was only available online or over the phone. Of course, I ran the entire city trying to find an office where I could speak to someone about our situation before I realized that just wasn't an option. All the facilities were designed for people to be able to use a computer to apply for benefits. They were not staffed with personnel that could assist you. I had expected to be able to make an appointment somewhere and sit down and speak with someone about getting everything changed over. Now I wasn't even sure which direction I needed to go. Do I call Medicaid, or do I contact the county? Exactly who files the necessary form?

It took me quite a few internet searches and phone calls to figure out which agency to contact. The first human being I could get through to that actually knew vaguely what I was talking about worked for Medicaid, and she said she couldn't help me. She directed me to contact my county. I had already tried the county but hadn't been able to get through to a real person. None of the automated categories fit the need for which I was calling, and the lines were always busy. The automated message told me to call back another time. Then the system would disconnect the call.

I found that the only way to get into the phone cue quick enough to be answered was to call the moment the office opened. Even so, I could still end up at the back of a long line of callers since everyone else seemed to have the same idea. Because our situation didn't fall under any of the automated phone categories that were offered, I would pick a category at random and hope for the best. I figured if I got to a real person, they could direct me to the correct department.

Unfortunately, that was not what happened. The staff answering the phones didn't have any idea what I was talking about. They spoke to me like I was an idiot. I had quite a few of them tell me that they don't offer any kind of medical assistance like that, and then they hung up on me. Calling back and being able to get in cue during the afternoon hours was near impossible. If I got hung up on, most likely it would be the next morning before I could get through again. All I could do was pray that a different person answered my call the next time I got through.

As new missionaries, Christopher and I were still in the process of raising a monthly support budget. Until we were fully funded financially, we both worked jobs in addition to serving at our mission agency. My available time to sit and make phone calls was limited. Sometimes I would sit on hold for over an hour until I finally had to hang up and clock in for my shift. When my shift ended, I would try again but would rarely be able to get through. If I did, I was hung up on or bounced around with no one able to help me.

In the meantime, I had already contacted the adoptive state to get everything prepared on their end, and they told me the exact steps that my new county needed to take to complete the agreement. They were so helpful that they even gave me the direct phone number to their adoption coordinator so that someone in my new county could speak to them directly if they had any questions. They assured me that setting up the agreement would be quick and easy. I was told that it was a fairly simple process that states initiate all the time. Supposedly, it takes no time at all to get it in place. No one in my county seemed to even know what it was.

Day after day, I called. It was a never-ending cycle of hold music and arguments with the voices on the other end of the line that kept telling me that what I was requesting wasn't real. My patience began to wear thin, and I started getting more and more aggressive. I demanded that they let me speak to a supervisor, but I was told over and over again that a supervisor was unavailable at that time. I needed to call back. Tears of frustration would be stinging my eyes at the end of each phone call because that meant another day was wasted.

Two months had already passed, and we were forced to begin rationing Thomas's medications. I could only do that for so long before they were gone. Time was ticking. I had already contacted every doctor's office within a fifty-mile radius of our new home, trying to get an appointment scheduled with a psychiatrist. Apparently, there was a major shortage of mental health professionals in our area. There was up to a six-month waiting list to get in to see one. None of them could write Thomas a prescription without seeing him first, and none of them would schedule him without proof of insurance.

I was told that the quickest way to get an appointment with a psychiatrist was to first start with a psychologist. The psychologist offices also had long waiting lists because their clients see the same limited number of psychiatrists. You couldn't see one without the other, and they too wanted to see proof of insurance. They would accept new patients who paid out of pocket, but there was no way we could afford the cost of the biweekly therapy sessions in addition to the medications. His medications were over $900 a month, and that was with generics. I was stuck. There was nothing more I could do but call again and pray that I get to someone who would be willing to listen. I desperately needed that insurance coverage.

With each passing day, we could see Thomas's mental state become more unstable and erratic. He became increasingly paranoid and started having psychotic episodes where he would pace and speak to things that weren't there. Everyone was on edge, waiting for something bad to happen. We didn't know what, but Thomas was barely holding on with all the upheaval and stress of a major move, a new school, new social situations, and not enough medication to help him maintain a stable sense of reality. It pained me to watch him struggle. I continually prayed for him to be able to hold on a little while longer.

His need is what continued to drive me to try again. Giving up was not an option. Eventually, I was able to get a supervisor on the line and explain my situation once again. She had never heard of an interstate agreement for insurance, but she assured me that she would look into it and get back with me. I made sure to get her direct phone number to follow up, and then I waited. When I didn't hear from her, I called and left her a message and prayed she wasn't going to be another dead end.

After three days, she finally called me back. She asked me to explain our situation to her one more time, and then she placed me on hold for what seemed like an eternity. She came back on the line and explained that she had found out that my request had made it to a case manager weeks ago. They didn't know what to do with it, so it was placed at the bottom of their pile and had been forgotten about. After a couple of hours of back and forth and being placed on hold while they contacted the adoption coordinator from his birth state, Thomas finally had insurance.

As soon as I ended that call, I contacted the psychiatrist's office to schedule an appointment. I was able to take a cancellation spot, but it was still two months away. I begged to be seen earlier. The scheduler assured me that there was no way to squeeze him in at any other time, even after I explained our dire situation. I reiterated to her that we didn't have two months. She said that unless my child harmed himself or someone else, there was nothing more that she could do. I'm sure the office gets calls from parents all the time trying to get appointments scheduled sooner rather than later. I had hoped to receive a little compassion, or at the very least some acknowledgment for my struggle, but instead she was abrupt and dismissive. We had no choice but to continue to pray and wait.

*****

After giving Thomas half doses and then cutting his half doses in half, he finally ran out of medication. We could see him slipping into a deeper state of psychosis with each passing day. Any attempts to engage with him or pull him back toward reality failed. I was desperate for time to go faster. His appointment wasn't scheduled until February; we had moved in September. The excitement of the Christmas season was providing him with something to occupy his thoughts, and with January being birthday month in our home, I was praying that the upcoming celebrations would help him hang on a little longer.

When the day arrived to celebrate our daughter's thirteenth birthday, we decided it was best to celebrate at home. I cooked one of our family's favorite meals and followed it up with our daughter's favorite flavor of cake and ice cream. It was good day full of laughter. Afterward, Thomas quickly retreated to his bedroom while the rest of us went to the living room to watch a movie together. Thomas chose to separate himself from the family. That was a typical behavior for him under normal circumstances and even more understandable with the struggle he was under to get through each day.

About halfway through the movie, Thomas came out of his bedroom with a towel wrapped around his neck and asked if he could take a shower. He never takes a shower without being coerced, and he has never ever asked to take one on his own before. Something just didn't seem right, and I could see that he was visibly shaken. When I pressed him about what was going on and why he had a towel wrapped around his neck, he moved it just enough for me to see deep purple bruises in the shape of rectangles.

I called his father over, and we started asking him what had happened. Thomas immediately started crying and admitted to hanging himself with his leather belt. He led us into his bedroom where he showed us a dark-green planter hook that we hadn't even noticed before that was screwed into the center of his window frame. The hook held strong, but thankfully his belt had snapped. He must have hung there for a little while with how deeply indented and bruised he was around his neck.

We immediately called 911, and within minutes, the police and an ambulance had arrived. They had shown up expecting to find a dead or near-dead child. The officers said they were relieved to see him shaken but sitting and talking with us on the couch. Thomas had just told us that the voices in his head had been relentless and that he just couldn't ignore them anymore. He said he was tired of fighting against them and decided to just give in to them telling him to kill himself. We could tell that going through with it had absolutely terrified him. The police radioed our local hospital to let them know that we were coming. They told us that they thought it would be less traumatic on Thomas if we drove him there ourselves.

When we arrived, the hospital staff had an emergency room waiting for us. They rushed us back through the double doors where doctors were already standing by, ready to examine him to make sure his neck hadn't been crushed or damaged in any way. They began asking him questions while they worked. Thomas answered all of them with a clarity and an honesty I had never seen him express before. His guard was down. While he answered their questions, his body started shaking, and tears began to stream down his cheeks. I could tell that his little body was in shock.

The hospital had already started the process of getting him admitted to the psychiatric floor. Thankfully, a bed had just opened up that evening, and it wasn't long before Thomas was swept upstairs and settled into his new room. After a very long intake process, they were able to get him fully admitted and scheduled him to see their staff psychiatrist first thing in the morning to start him back on all of his medications.

Before we left the hospital that night, we had to sit Thomas down and explain to him that we had to leave him there and that we couldn't stay with him. He didn't fully understand exactly where he was, and when he realized we were going to leave him in the room alone, he started to cry again. He was scared, and he looked up at us and said, "But I'm just a little boy, and I'm supposed to be home with my mommy and daddy." Both of us immediately teared up. He had never spoken of us in that way before, and that simple revelation pierced our hearts.

That was the first time Thomas had ever expressed a need for either one of us in the seven years since he had come to live with us. We had caught a glimpse of how vulnerable he felt in that moment before his guard was back in place. We assured him that we would be back in the morning with some clean clothes and that we would see him then. It was difficult to hear the doors to the secure wing latch behind us. It felt like we were abandoning him at such a difficult time, but he was exactly where he needed to be.

We went home that evening in shock of what could have been. Thomas had frightened himself enough to finally open up to the doctors about how much he had been struggling. There was no indication that he had planned to harm himself that evening. I don't think there was anything different we could have done as a family. We were just thankful that the belt had broken. I didn't want to dwell on the outcome if it would have held.

The scheduler's voice at the psychiatrist's office kept running through my mind, telling me that unless he harms himself or someone else, there was nothing more they could do. Well, he harmed himself! My shock quickly turned to anger. I was furious, not with Thomas but at the whole situation. I had done everything I could have done, but it wasn't enough. All of those hours I spent on hold and begging for assistance. All of the people I had spoken with— argued with—to get the help that I needed.

That evening was completely avoidable. It didn't have to come to that. Thomas shouldn't have had to suffer day after day, struggling to resist those voices. What in the world would we have done if we would have found him hanging there the next morning? I dared to not dwell on that, but instead I spent the evening praising the Lord that his belt had snapped when there was no reason for it not to have held. I am convinced that it is only through our continued prayers that he survived.

Thomas stayed at the hospital for seven days. He was placed back on all of his prescriptions, and the doctor wanted to give it some time for them to build up in his system before releasing him. He wanted some assurance from Thomas that he wasn't going to try to kill himself again. They would have kept him longer, but his birthday was exactly one week after his sister's. We didn't want him to spend his birthday alone. His doctor agreed that it would be best to go ahead and release him early so that he came back home to a celebration. It was already evident that the few days of medications had begun to make a difference in his countenance. He was slowly improving with each day. He turned twelve the morning we brought him home.

CHAPTER 10

For God has not given us a spirit of fear,
but of power and of love and of a sound mind.
—2 Timothy 1:7

After Thomas's attempted suicide, things were never quite the same. We started watching his behaviors more closely than we already had been. We wanted to be sure to catch any indication of him attempting to take his own life again. We knew that as long as those voices were there, the temptation to give in to them was also present. Thomas learned quickly that hearing voices was not considered normal, and whether or not he heard them became a regular topic of conversation with his new psychiatrist.

The more Thomas was asked about them, the more paranoid he became and the more he denied ever hearing them in the first place. We knew he was still hearing them because we would catch him having conversations with them whenever he thought we weren't listening. The voices didn't seem to try to hide anymore, and at night, his sister could hear him having full conversations with them through their shared wall.

The voices were relentless in convincing Thomas that we were against him and that we hated him. He grew increasingly paranoid of our intentions toward him with each passing day. Within six weeks of him being discharged from the hospital, Thomas had a mental breakdown and went running and screaming down our street. Our oldest son, Jacob, chased him down and tackled him in the grass. Dad was right behind, and together they restrained him while I called the police. Within minutes, they had arrived, and Thomas was put in the back of the police car.

Neighbors came out onto their porches to watch us when they heard the ruckus the saw the flashing lights. Some of our neighbors felt it was okay to start yelling at us and accusing us of trying to harm him. One man, in particular, started recording us with his cell phone while threatening to post the video to YouTube. He was threatening to report us for child abuse.

One of the police officers told him to stop heckling us and to go back inside his house. The man refused and started arguing with the officer. The officer had to threaten to pull his gun and arrest the man before he would comply. Our neighbor was told that if the video ever made it to YouTube, the police would come back to his home and arrest him. Thomas spent the next five days in a mental health facility.

Only about 1 percent of the world's population will develop schizophrenia. Anyone can develop the condition, but it is extremely rare in children before the age of twelve. It was listed among Thomas's diagnoses when he was only ten years old. Doctors say schizophrenia is suspected to develop from factors such as genetics and nervous system development, to low oxygen levels during childbirth, and possible exposure to a virus during infancy.

Early loss or separation from a parent, as well as verbal, physical, or sexual abuse in adolescence is also considered to be contributing factors. In my experience, those seem to be much more likely, but the cause remains a much debated subject among professionals. It doesn't seem to me that medical professionals really know, or at least no one can come to a clear consensus, of why it happens, only that it can happen. One thing that researchers can agree upon is that it is as varied and as complicated a condition as its symptoms.

Eugen Bleuler coined the term *schizophrenia* in 1908, which literally means a split or fracturing of the mind. Individuals with schizophrenia completely lose touch with reality. They are prone to paranoid delusions where they believe everyone is out to cause them harm, which can lead them to display irrational beliefs that manifest through very abnormal behaviors. On the other hand, they can have delusions of grandeur where they believe that they can fly, or that they are a genius, or that they are famous.

Schizophrenics have hallucinations which include hearing sounds or voices that aren't really there. Sometimes there are multiple voices that speak directly to the person, or the voices can speak to just each other, but the person can still hear them and be influenced by them. The voices tend to be very critical and encourage the person to do things that they wouldn't normally do—like hang themselves. Schizophrenia is a lifelong condition, but with the proper medication and treatment, doctors say some quality of life can be maintained. Doctors also say the earlier it is diagnosed, the more successful treatment can be.

However, maintaining a long-term treatment plan for schizophrenics is very difficult because they would have to accept their need for intervention and treatment in the first place. This can be a challenge if they are paranoid of the doctors, the exams, or of the medications they are given. Treatment of the condition is also very individualized. Treatment plans are based upon the specific symptoms that each individual displays continually over a long period of time. There is no one-plan-fits-all option. Finding the right blend of medications takes an extended period of time.

Regulating their medications is usually a lot of trial and error with regular adjustments as the body builds up a tolerance for them. The psychotropic drugs that are prescribed affect the central nervous system, altering the brain's chemistry in effort to improve the individual's mood. Some medications can work well while others can make the person very sick.

When a blend is found that works well, the person can begin to gain some control over their thoughts and can start feeling more balanced emotionally. Once they start feeling good, it is common for them to decide that they no longer have a need to take the medication. So they often quit taking them and then slip right back into a psychotic state again.

Maintaining their daily med management can be a challenge for them and especially for a caregiver. It can easily become the object of contention between the two, which was my daily struggle with Thomas. I would find his pills hidden all over his bedroom and sometimes in the corners of the living room or kitchen floors. You could tell that most of them had been in his mouth for a moment and had begun to slightly dissolve.

It usually took some erratic behavior to prompt one of us to search the house for pills, but it was always pretty easy to confirm that he had been spitting them out. We learned to have him take his medication in front of us and open his mouth nice and wide to prove to us that he had swallowed them. Unfortunately, this kind of follow-through just increased his perception that we were trying to control him and force him to do things he didn't want to do.

*****

Looking back at Thomas's behavior when he was around ten and eleven years old, I can identify some schizophrenic tendencies. Those earlier tendencies manifested with delusions of grandeur. One time, he and I went to pick up his siblings from their homeschool co-op that met in a large church building. At the end of the day, all the students, about two hundred of them, gathered in the gymnasium and grouped together by class where they would wait with their teachers until their parents arrived to release them.

On this one particular afternoon, the security system was being tested, and although the alarm had been silenced, the security lights posted around the gymnasium were flashing at regular intervals. The lights were blinding, but the hustle and bustle of the room continued unaffected as parents arrived to check out their children. Since we had to go to three different class groups, Thomas and I had to squeeze our way back and forth through the crowd. Once we were all present, I turned around to make sure Thomas was still with me before heading toward the door.

When I stopped walking to watch him, so did the other kids, and together we froze in amazement. Thomas was standing in the center of the gymnasium with people chatting and moving all around him. No one else was paying him any attention, but there he stood smiling and striking a new pose with each flash of the lights. For one flash, he gave a thumbs-up and then quickly shifted into a Superman pose for the next. On and on, he changed what he was doing for each new flash. His poses were imaginative and hilarious, and the four of us just stood there laughing. He was fully engaged and completely committed to his very own personal photo shoot.

Later that evening when his father came home, he excitedly ran up to him to tell him that someone had been in the gym earlier that day to take his picture. He was convinced that he had been the subject of a real photo shoot. He had somehow lost the awareness that anyone else had been in the room with him—although it was practically shoulder-to-shoulder crowded at the time. His siblings tried all day long to explain to him why the lights had been flashing, but he remained positive that they were flashing for him and him alone.

He was also convinced, for a short season, that the world was at his feet. He would turn just about anything into a microphone, and then he was instantly transported on stage with a crowd of screaming fans before him. Broomsticks became guitars, and whatever music happened to be playing at the time instantly became his own personal soundtrack.

It didn't seem to matter where we were or what was happening around him. The rest of the world simply disappeared. During those times, he would seem to be putting on a full concert. He would work the room, shake imaginary hands, and receive standing ovations. In a way, it was refreshing to see him passionate and fully invested in something. It was nice to see a smile on his face, even if it was only due to his imaginary fans.

By the time he was nearing twelve, puberty was in full swing. His psychosis continued to increase, and his view of himself and the world around him began to shift. Instead of seeing himself on top of the world, he started feeling like the world was out to get him. It was as if his imaginary audience had started turning against him. Having to uproot the family and move to a new state hadn't helped the situation either. All the change seemed to compound his struggles. At that time, all of us were suffering from culture shock and loneliness. The transition was much more difficult than any of us had expected.

It wasn't long after Thomas came home from the hospital that I started finding notes around his room that he had written to himself. The notes were usually step-by-step instructions in the form of checklists with open boxes where he could check each item off as he completed them. He created detailed plans of how he was going to sneak around the house at night and search through our bedrooms for things he wanted. He wrote plans of how he was going to play video games all night long without being caught.

He wrote himself reminders to "secrets" he had uncovered about his brother Isaiah in hopes of getting him in trouble, which seemed to be a consistent goal for him. He even wrote a note about how much he wanted to run away but concluded at the bottom of it that he was a coward. He knew he didn't have the courage to follow through with it just yet. We figured him running away was just a matter of time.

Thomas would lie in his bed for hours filing up page after page with rap lyrics about girls, doing drugs, and becoming notoriously rich and famous. He would make up whole scenarios of different lives he would lead and how amazing everything would one day become. He would write about his riches and how we would one day come to him in our desperation to beg him for money. He wrote about how he would turn us away and then revel in our poverty and despair.

Thomas's social life became strained as he started getting into fights at school and with the other kids in our neighborhood. He made lists of who had it out for him and who he was going to round up to help him fight back. At one point, the teens in our neighborhood had split into two different gangs. They walked the neighborhood in packs and regularly fought one another.

Due to his cowardice, Thomas didn't usually go at things head-on. He schemed and plotted behind the scenes, riling everyone else up around him. He would much rather flee and avoid a conflict than face it head-on all by himself, but with friends rallied behind him, he became quite brave and usually spoke with the loudest voice.

Sometimes their conflicts would get so bad that Thomas would hide in the house for fear of the other gang's retaliation from something he and his cohorts had done. On a few occasions, the two groups ended up posturing and yelling at each other on our street corner. I kept an eye out, but it never seemed to escalate into anything too serious. It was all foolishness. It was obvious that Thomas was stirring up trouble wherever he went.

Thomas viewed school as a punishment and an intrusion to his life. By the time he was in middle school, he did everything he could think of to avoid it. We started getting automated phone calls in the evenings letting us know that our student had skipped a class or two that day. When we would confront him that evening and ask him where he had been, he would act shocked at the accusation and say that the school was lying.

When he knew we weren't convinced, he was quick to come up with a reason for the school's error in reporting his attendance. After all, he was only tardy and missed the teacher taking attendance because he was in the restroom. The substitute teacher didn't even take attendance that day, or he was in the library studying. He went to see the nurse because his stomach was upset—even though there was never a nurse kept on-site.

My favorite excuse was that his teacher sent him to make up some standardized testing he had missed. They must have forgotten to mark him present for the day. If he was in class every day, then how come he kept missing all those testing times? We told him that he must be the smartest student in the whole school with all the hours of testing he had been doing. He didn't appreciate that comment and just assumed we were calling him stupid. He was so angry that he didn't speak to either of us for days.

*****

Thomas changed to a new therapist, and he wasted no time at all in informing her of how abusive we were being toward him. He was convinced that by making him go to school every day, we were actually abusing him. Making him do any kind of household chore that he didn't want to do was also considered abusive in his mind. The only chore he wanted to do was sweeping and organizing the front porch. If you asked for anything more, you were just being cruel.

Basically, anything he didn't want to do was placed in the abuse category. Even though it was explained to him over and over again that cleaning his room, helping wash dishes after dinner, and going to school every day was what was normally expected of children his age, he just wouldn't accept it as truth. In his mind, everyone was out to make his life miserable, and his teachers were especially out to get him above everyone else. They put demands on him to participate in class. He didn't like that they were constantly telling him what he could and could not do. He was angry that he wasn't allowed to leave class whenever he wanted or that he couldn't put his head down on his desk and sleep until the bell rang. Expecting him to complete his assignments was an unreasonable expectation.

Most mornings, he would try to refuse to get out of bed, or he would move as slowly as possible so that I would be forced to leave him behind in order to get myself to work on time. Sometimes he would deliberately run out of clean clothes so that he could say that he couldn't go to school because he had nothing clean to wear. Whenever that was the excuse, I would have to tell him that he should have planned ahead. Then I would have to insist he choose something to wear from his floor and then stand there as patiently as I could until he picked something up and put it on.

Waiting for him to make up his mind to comply was an excruciatingly long process. Once he realized his excuses weren't going to garner any of the results he was looking for, he would get dressed in clothes that didn't look any better or worse than anything else he chose to wear on any other given day. He would move as slowly as possible and then reluctantly get in the car.

Our car rides to school were always tenuous. He would refuse to look at me and his father or acknowledge us in any way. On the days where he tried everything he could think of to get out of going—which was most days—his anger toward us would seem to be seething from his pores. Inevitably, he would slam the car door as hard as he could to make sure we knew exactly how he felt, although not a word had been spoken between us.

We made sure to meet with Thomas's teachers at the beginning of a new school year to introduce ourselves and to explain his history, his suicide attempt, and to make them aware of certain behaviors and issues that they should watch out for. We set up a contact protocol for them to reach us directly because giving Thomas notes or report cards to carry home never worked. Whatever he was given always disappeared before he made it home in the evenings.

One time, a teenager we knew who lived at the end of our street noticed a piece of pink paper crumpled up and shoved into the fire hydrant on her corner. When she pulled it out, she recognized Thomas's name and walked it down to our house. He was sure that he had discarded his progress report successfully. He was shocked to see that it had ended up in our hands.

Thankfully, most of his teachers were very accommodating to our need for alternative communication. They would e-mail or call us to let us know what lessons they were doing in class and what assignments and projects he was currently required to complete. Sometimes we would have to read the teacher's e-mails out loud to him or show him the notices about missing assignments that had been mailed directly to our home before he would stop trying to convince us that his teachers never gave him any work to do or that he was turning everything in during class.

He would still refuse to complete the assignments, but he knew we knew, and he eventually stopped working so hard to lie to us about it. His response to our questions about how he was doing, what he was learning, or where he was during second period was now answered with complete silence. He believed he didn't owe us a response, and he said we had no right to ask him questions and no right to know the answers.

He felt betrayed by his teacher's direct communication. His overall hostility toward us for trying to parent him and tell him what to do continued to rise. His disdain for school seemed to increase with each passing month. He was only in the seventh grade. He had five and a half more years to go. I started becoming concerned that he wasn't going to make it through junior high, let alone high school. My hope of him ever graduating began to wane.

CHAPTER 11

Though they plot evil against you and
devise wicked schemes, they cannot succeed.
—Psalm 21:11

When we arrived, the school was swarming with activity. The detective refused to tell us what had happened over the phone, but he requested that we get to the school as quickly as possible. During the ride there, my heart was pounding. Something bad must have happened for a detective to call. We couldn't even begin to speculate what it might be.

We were immediately ushered into a large conference room that was packed full of what appeared to be local and district school administrators and uniformed police detectives. There were two chairs reserved for us at one end of the table, but other than that, it was standing room only.

After we took our seats, the person at the head of the table introduced themselves as the school principal, and then she proceeded to ask us questions about Thomas. Had he been acting suspicious lately? Were we aware of any issues or anger he had toward his teachers? Was he having problems with any other students? We explained to the room Thomas's diagnoses and his struggles with school, but we assured them that we hadn't noticed any alarming behavior that was outside of the norm for him.

We were then informed that earlier that morning, one of Thomas's teachers had intercepted a note that he was passing back and forth with another student. In that note was a detailed plan they were calling "zero day." Apparently, he and two other boys were planning to set off bombs in the school and then murder their teachers.

The teacher immediately notified the principal, and detectives were called to the school. Each of the boys were quietly removed from class and questioned independently.

We learned that Thomas had been stealing bomb-making supplies from neighboring houses and then taking them to school so that one of the other boys could assemble the bombs that he had learned how to make from the internet. These boys had drawn a map of where they were going to hide each of the bombs. They listed specific details of how they were going to detonate them and then kill their teachers in the aftermath of the explosions.

Christopher collected ancient weaponry that was displayed around our bedroom. While Thomas was being questioned, he admitted that one of his roles was to sneak his father's battle axe to the school so that he could be the one to "hack up" the teachers. Needless to say, those items were quickly removed from our home later that evening and stored at a friend's house indefinitely.

We had no idea that Thomas was capable of plotting something that violent. We knew he hated school and did whatever he could to get out of going, but we never would have dreamed of him being a part of something so serious. One of the scariest things to me was that he didn't seem to understand what the big deal was. It didn't appear that he understood why he was being questioned, which would mean he in no way understood the gravity of what he was involved in.

After we left the conference room, we sat in the hallway with Thomas and the detective who had been questioning him. The detective said that Thomas had told him that he was adopted. He then pointed out the eczema on Thomas's arms and said that he had accused us of beating him and had claimed that his eczema rashes were scars from the abuse. The officer was quick to say that he recognized the eczema. He knew that Thomas was lying right away. He said he had suspected there were some mental disabilities at work, and he was eager to speak with us and get some clarification.

After we spent some time answering questions about ourselves and our family, the detective said that Thomas was free to go home. He had decided that because we were ordained ministers and because of our "station within the community," they had decided not to press charges. We thanked him for his consideration, but we actually requested that they press charges anyway. He continued to insist that they didn't want to do that to our family.

Up until this point, Thomas's rage had been directed toward us and not outward toward other people. If he was starting to escalate, we needed documentation so that we could get him additional mental health services. Our concerns leading up to this point seemed to be dismissed by his therapist. This was exactly what we needed documented to be able to take the necessary steps to protect ourselves, our other children, and now the rest of society.

The detective didn't believe that Thomas was mentally capable of being the instigator and coming up with the bomb plot on his own. He and the other detectives were convinced that Thomas had been manipulated to participate, but I'm not sure that he was so blindly innocent. No one else knew that his father owned a battle axe. At the very least, he willingly offered that piece of information and then agreed to bring it to the school to further their cause.

I agree he would have needed help to craft such an intricate plan, but hearing about a revenge plot against the school and his teachers, that seemed like something that could be right up his alley. The detective assured us that the other boys involved were being dealt with—whatever that means. It seemed like their main objective was to keep the incident quiet and out of the press.

The most important thing was that the plan was thwarted. It would have been helpful for us if Thomas would have been charged, or we would have a least been given some sort of documentation of the incident. No notifications were sent home to any of the parents, and the school day continued as if nothing sinister had been in play. The other students in the school, including our own daughter, were completely unaware of the day's events. After a short vacation (I mean suspension), Thomas was back to his regular routine of sleeping through class, refusing to participate, and skipping at least one class period per day.

It was terrifying to think that our child could have helped orchestrate an attack on a school where lives could have been lost. Until now, his violence seemed to be directed toward us and us alone.

We were having some sort of physical altercation with him two to three times a week where he would kick us or use household items as weapons against us. I had wondered if he would escalate later in life and find himself in prison for something, but I never once expected him to be involved in anything like this and at such a young age. He was only thirteen years old. It was in that moment that the potential threat that he posed to society became very real.

By the end of that school year, Thomas was not only physically fighting with us but was now repeatedly threatening to murder all of us in our sleep. Maybe I wouldn't have taken his threats so seriously before, but after recent events, I wasn't going to dismiss them. I replaced all of our bedroom doorknobs so that each of us could lock ourselves into our rooms at night. This was the only way that I could think of to protect ourselves while we slept.

A new fear settled into our home, which increased my prayers and petitions to God for protection. I refused to let fear take hold of me, but there was now a real and tangible threat living with us. In the mornings, I never knew if we would wake up to a dead child where Thomas had killed himself or, even worse, murdered one of the others in the middle of the night. In that instance, we would lose two children. Unthinkable.

Adding the locks to our bedroom doors only seemed to magnify Thomas's paranoia. He was convinced that we were hiding something from him instead of realizing that we were locking our doors to protect ourselves and our belongings. He had been stealing from us for months now: jewelry, money, phones, video games, headphones, thumb drives—you name it. With the added threats being made against us personally, the locks had become a necessity.

Everyone carried their own key to their bedroom door. Christopher and I carried keys to all of them. If one of us accidentally left our keys sitting out somewhere in the house, they would quickly vanish. If they didn't turn up within a few days, I would have to replace all the doorknobs so that the keys he stole no longer worked. Thomas was so obsessed with finding keys that one morning while we were away, he kicked down our bedroom door so that he could search our room for a master set. He knew that if he could get his hands on our keys, no room in the house would be off-limits.

Thomas damaged most of our windows by forcing them open on mornings where he skipped school and came home to search the house while everyone else was away. He helped himself to anything in the house that he could trade or sell for cash. Sometimes it would take us a few days to figure out what he had stolen versus what might have been misplaced by one of us. Breaking into our bedrooms didn't only happen while we were away. Isaiah has woken up to Thomas standing over him in the middle of the night on more than one occasion.

*****

Thomas spent as much time as possible that summer sleeping in or hanging out with a neighbor boy whom he had become friends with during the previous school year. Thomas would leave the house most days without saying a word. Sometimes I would think he was still in his bed but would discover that he had actually climbed out of his bedroom window without any of us noticing.

He avoided contact with the family as much as possible, and whenever one of us would ask what he had been up to, he would shrug his shoulders and maybe give a vague "nothin'" response. I was very suspicious of what he was doing especially with the way he was avoiding us and sneaking around. I just knew he was up to no good, but there wasn't anything blatant going on that I could pinpoint. I just didn't trust him.

Every now and then, I would ask our older boys to check in with the neighbor to see if they could find out anything about Thomas. Although the neighbor boy was friends with Thomas, he didn't seem to shy away from telling on him whenever they asked. They had to be careful and not too pushy, but a simple conversation usually confirmed my suspicions.

Since the neighbor boy had a lot of freedom and not a lot of parental oversight, he did all sorts of things that I would never have allowed Thomas to do such as smoke pot. He introduced smoking to him in seventh grade, and it wasn't long before they were smoking together almost every day. We have found videos on Facebook of Thomas sitting in the neighbor's shed laughing and blowing smoke rings. I guess if he's going to do drugs, I would rather him smoke pot than anything else. I had also heard that they were experimenting with mushrooms. I could only hope that their experimenting wouldn't escalate any further.

I tried my best to limit the boys' time together, but they were pretty much inseparable. Thomas seemed obsessed with him, and if I forbade him from going to his house, there was all-out war, or he would walk out the front door and go anyway. It was easier just to let him go than to deal with the fallout. Thomas figured out quickly that I was trying to limit their time together. Instead of asking if he could go next door, he would say that he wanted to go the park or ride his bike instead. I always knew what his real intention was, and sure enough, that's where he would end up every single time.

The neighbor boy verified that Thomas had been banned from the corner store for stealing. His bedroom had become littered with food wrappers and soda bottles for some time. When I would ask him where he got them, Thomas always claimed that a friend had bought them for him. I know that the neighbor did on occasion. His divorced parents seemed to be fairly absent in his life, but they always made sure he had plenty of money in his pocket. Even so, it is rare to have friends so young be quite so generous.

Unfortunately, stealing wasn't limited to the corner store. We found out that Thomas had been breaking into neighborhood garages and stealing random items like shovels and flashlights, anything that seemed enticing in the moment. Isaiah went behind him and put some of the items back if he managed to find out which home they belonged to. I expected for a neighbor to come knocking on our door any day, but none ever came. Somehow both boys managed to go undetected.

I really hoped that Thomas would get caught in the act because he needed some consequences before his criminal behavior became a lifestyle. On the flip side, I hoped that his brother wouldn't get caught since he was only trying to undo what Thomas had done because it shamed and embarrassed him. That shame wasn't his to carry. He was trying his best to protect the family and to protect his parents' reputation most of all.

We also learned that Thomas had been throwing rocks at cars while they would drive down our street and that he had been known to rummage through parked cars looking for change or anything seemingly worthy of being taken. It became evident that if Thomas has decided that he wants something, he simply takes it. It doesn't really matter where we are or who is around; items simply disappear in his presence.

Late one evening, a mother and her daughter that we knew from church showed up on our doorstep following a youth service. The teenage girl had left her purse sitting to the side of the room that night. Inside her purse was a brand-new iPhone that she had worked hard to purchase with her own money that she had saved for months. Many of the teenagers ended up searching the church that night shortly after she had noticed that her phone had gone missing.

Unfortunately, the phone had died and powered off. Otherwise, she would have been able to ping its location to find out where it was. Some of the other teens said that they saw Thomas and another boy near the purse that evening, but when they were questioned, they both denied that they had taken it. Naturally, the girl was furious and heartbroken. They came to our house to see if we could search Thomas and his bedroom. She was convinced that he had stolen it.

We searched everywhere while they waited, but we didn't find the phone. Thomas was indignant throughout the whole process. We encouraged them to call the police since the phone was such an expensive item, and within minutes, the police were at our door. We stood outside while they questioned Thomas on our front steps. Everyone present, including the police officers, believed he was guilty, but since the phone hadn't turned up, it was word against word with no evidence. The police were unable to do anything other than lecture him and try to get him to admit to the theft, which he claimed he didn't do.

We gave the police the other boy's name and address. They went to his house as well that night, but the other boy said he didn't have it either. We learned that his family was moving the following morning. That evening had been his last night at youth group. We were told that the two boys wanted to stay in contact with each other and had been discussing how they were going to do that at the church. We surmise that Thomas took the phone and gave it to his friend so that they could stay in contact with each other. Maybe they stole it together. We will never know.

What we do know is that the phone never turned up and was never powered on again. We didn't have any iPhone chargers in our home, but one of the teenagers "left" a charger behind, hoping that if Thomas had the phone, he would try to charge it and use it. If it made it to his friend's house, maybe it scared him to have the police show up asking about it. If it was stashed in the church somewhere to be reclaimed at a later time, it never turned up again. Maybe one of them dumped it somewhere. Unfortunately, we will never know what truly happened that night.

*****

One of my husband's favorite scriptures is Numbers 32:23, which says, "Be sure your sin will find you out." That is something he has quoted to our children all of their lives. We knew that if Thomas or any of our children were to start sneaking or misbehaving, it would eventually come to light. We have seen the truth of this scripture work to our advantage over and over again to the point that our older sons started telling on themselves whenever they did something wrong because they knew Dad would find out anyway.

When we joined our church, we felt it was only appropriate to speak to both the children's pastor and the youth pastor so that they were aware of our family dynamics and the specific challenges we face with Thomas. It wouldn't be right to just drop him off without letting them know what to look out for. We didn't want them to be blindsided with any malbehaviors. We never knew what Thomas was going to do from day to day, and if they were going to be watching over him and pastoring him, we felt that it was only right to give them a heads-up.

When we introduced ourselves and tried to share a little bit about Thomas, we felt immediately dismissed. It was evident that we were not being taken seriously. One of the leaders asked what medications he was taking and then proceeded to argue with us that we must be mistaken because those medications are not prescribed to children. Another began to lecture us on how to parent him even though they were not a parent themselves, and they didn't have any understanding of adoption issues or mental illness.

They went on to say that all we needed to do was love Thomas and hug on him—as if we had never thought of that before. They said that if we did that, everything would simply work itself out. Love overcomes a lot of things, but love isn't just soft and tender hugs. Love can also be firm and corrective. Love was not letting your child do whatever they wanted. Ignoring any future issues wouldn't be beneficial to either party. We were only sharing a snapshot of our experiences with them for their own benefit. We didn't want Thomas causing problems and them not knowing how to handle it.

We weren't asking the pastors to do anything other than to let us know immediately if they notice anything out of the ordinary. That was it. We weren't asking them to discipline him or change anything to accommodate him. We felt that if they were going to be interacting with Thomas week in and week out, teaching him and ministering to him, they needed to understand him and be able to recognize any of his unhealthy or destructive behaviors.

Spiritual leaders should be well educated about disabilities and mental illness. Too few churches have programs equipped to assist families like ours that don't fit the typical mold. Unless there has been some specialized training, or someone on staff has a family member with disabilities, there doesn't seem to be an understanding of the needs and support that could be helpful for a family like ours. Even so, every situation, every family, every child is unique, which means their needs are unique. I believe each child is worthy of care and support in those spiritual environments as a direct representation of God's love.

It is vital that any support that is offered be made available to the whole family, not just the one with special needs. It would have been wonderful for our other children to have had someone who cared enough to invest in them on an intimate level. Someone in whom they could confide that would really listen to them without dismissing their struggles. We have found that, more often than not, church leaders simply offer the customary Sunday school responses when they don't know what to say. Telling teenagers to give it to the Lord or pray about it isn't wrong, but it isn't helpful either.

Dismissing my children's struggles with their brother as being typical sibling issues teaches them that it is not safe to open up about what they are facing. Even normal, everyday sibling conflicts can be hurtful and damaging. How much more are their struggles intensified when there is a genuine fear for their safety? Not having that safe place to share how they are truly feeling has left them feeling alone and isolated around their peers. Depression, anxiety, and any thoughts of suicide are then stuffed and dealt with internally where they fester and grow stronger.

Our family is very selective with whom we will open up with about Thomas. It's not that we are hiding anything or that we don't want to talk about it. We've just learned that it is often more damaging to be vulnerable and then dismissed, not believed, or lectured on how we should be handling it or feeling about it than keeping it to ourselves. It seems that some people we know have only asked how things were going because they wanted to know the latest gossip. Their inquiries were not made from a place of genuine care but curiosity. In those instances, I will shut down and tell you as little as possible. What my family needs is a listening ear and someone who will simply pray with us.

My daughter was very hurt by her leaders that told her that she was exaggerating or that she just needed to pray about how she was feeling without investing any time to help her through her struggles. She has told me that she will scream the next time someone tells her that they understand how she feels because their best friend's, aunt's daughter adopted, and they learned that they just had to love the child. Hearing about adoption struggles is not the same as living it. She says the worst is when someone looks at her and says, "Poor

Thomas." She immediately thinks, *Poor Thomas? What about poor Michal? I'm the one who has to live with him!*

We know that people are trying to be helpful and understanding in their own way, but if I could share a bit of wisdom here, it is always best to just listen. Unsolicited advice is rarely beneficial. Trust me when I say that whatever you think of to say in that moment has already been thought of or said by someone else. Unless it is a direct prophetic word from heaven, it's best to just cry along with us and tell us that you're here for us to talk to whenever we need a listening ear. That's all that most people really need anyway.

After we informed the leadership, my husband and I walked away, thinking that the truth will eventually come to light. Apparently, they were going to have to experience it to believe it. Fast-forward, and we find out that Thomas has been messing with the knobs on the soundboards, changing passwords on the computers, and climbing up into the speaker bays after being told repeatedly not to do so.

Thomas was seen looking at porn on his phone in the middle of a youth service, and he would often disappear where no one would be able to find him for extended periods of time. We eventually found out that he was roaming the church halls or leaving the church building and walking around in the dark doing who knows what. Thomas was often not where he was supposed to be, doing what he was not supposed to be doing.

Part of the church building used to be a school, and Thomas had been caught climbing through the ceiling tiles into locked rooms numerous times. There is no telling how many offices or classrooms he climbed into or what he did once he got in. We learned that one of his most frequented rooms was the youth's snack shack. That would explain all of the times I've seen him walking the halls on a Sunday morning sipping on a soda and munching on candy.

Since Thomas had difficulty sitting through the Sunday morning service with the rest of the teenagers, he had asked to help out in kids' church instead. Thomas does great with younger children, so I agreed. I hoped it would be beneficial for him to be with the younger ones since his understanding was at a lower level than his peers, and he didn't know many of the Bible stories you typically learn in kids' church. He was in class every week, but it wasn't long before we heard that he was causing more disruption for the teacher than actually helping.

One Sunday, while we were on our way home from church, we were told that offering money had gone missing and that Thomas was the main suspect. We ended up stripping Thomas down to his underwear on the front porch before we would allow him to go into the house. We didn't want him to have an opportunity to hide what he had possibly stolen. We didn't want to assume that he was the culprit or have every suspicious situation immediately directed toward him, but experience had taught us to fully investigate. We didn't recover any of the monies, and no one knew for sure if he had taken it; but after that morning, he was asked to not return to the children's ministry again.

About a year later, one of the church leaders sat down with Thomas to inform him that he was no longer allowed to attend the youth group. Up until then, most of what we were hearing was coming from his siblings or from the gossip of other members of the church. None of the leadership had ever approached us about anything. Thomas felt blindsided. He doesn't remember what he does one minute to the next. He is especially unaware of how his actions might be affecting others. It was shocking to him to have been kicked out without warning. He left that meeting quite upset.

Thomas probably would have ended up being kicked out of youth either way, but it would have been better if we had been informed of all the things he was doing as he did them. That is what we had asked for from the very beginning. We might have been able to help. At the very least, he would have been disciplined along the way, and maybe the sudden expulsion wouldn't have been as unexpected.

From the very first week, we started stopping by the youth services unannounced to make sure that Thomas was behaving himself and listening to the adults. Whenever we would ask how he was doing, the leaders always assured us that he was doing just fine. His siblings watched him like a hawk, and they were constantly annoyed by every little thing that he did. He couldn't breathe without one of them being frustrated or embarrassed by something he had done, but he didn't seem to be bothering the leaders, so we let him continue going.

We would rarely have to ask the others how Thomas was doing each week because the first thing they did when they got home was run down a list. Thomas's little quirks and subtle defiance were ruining their ability to enjoy themselves. Eventually, they took my advice and started ignoring him. If no one else was being bothered by the little things that he was doing, then they needed to stop stressing about it and just enjoy their time with their friends.

As things got more difficult at home, they didn't want to have to think about him, watch him, or correct him in any way during their youth gatherings. They did their best to ignore him and keep their distance so that the leadership could handle anything that came up. The older ones told me once that when a new student joined the group, they did everything they could to not let them know that Thomas was their brother. They wanted that fact to remain a secret for as long as possible. They just wanted to pretend that life was normal for a few hours each week.

There were many times that the three of them begged us to forbid Thomas from going to youth at all. We did keep him home on occasion, but when he stayed home with us, he would be miserable, which would make us miserable. Thomas didn't want to be home with us. He would either hide in his room or end up at the neighbor's house running around or playing video games all night.

Youth was the only positive environment Thomas actually wanted to be in. It was the only safe place where he could go to play games and invite his friend to come along. It was also the only place he was willing to go where someone was teaching about Jesus. He wasn't open to learning about the Gospel from his family. How could we deny him the only opportunity he had to learn about God? I'd rather him be running around and playing at the church than running the streets at home.

I wish there would have been some other option that would have worked where no one's need would have had to have been sacrificed. It took a while, but eventually our older children got their wish. Thomas was kicked out of both the children's and the youth ministry. They were happier, the youth group was probably better for it, and Thomas found other things to occupy his time. With his refusal to participate in Sunday morning serves, there was no other option available for him to remain as an active member within the church community.

CHAPTER 12

We are hard pressed on every side,
but not crushed; perplexed, but not in despair.
—2 Corinthians 4:8

Thomas was advanced to eighth grade, although he didn't earn the grades to be promoted with only having a 1.69 GPA. We began the school year hopeful that it would at least be better than the year before. We set up our usual introductory meeting with his teachers to briefly explain his history and some of his previous behaviors that may affect his success throughout the upcoming school year.

Thomas, being in the same school, was already familiar with the routine of the school day. He had well established hiding places, and he knew the surrounding neighborhood and how to navigate his way to and from our home with ease. His sister had advanced to high school, and he took every advantage of not having a sibling around to verify whether or not he stayed on campus.

He attended his new classes long enough to learn which rooms they were in, who his teachers were, and whether or not he had someone interesting to sit next to. Within no time, the automated attendance messages started ringing every evening at six o'clock, informing us that our student had skipped class that day. Our hopes of a better, more productive year quickly faded.

When we relocated, our new state informed us that we would not be able to benefit from any of the services that would normally be made available to adoptive families since we adopted Thomas out of state. If we had been offered some kind of assistance or at least been given a contact person that could have been available to answer questions, I believe our initial difficulties surrounding our transition could have been avoided.

We had spent the past two years trying to navigate his care completely on our own, and we quickly learned that without the proper connections and referrals, there were very limited resources made available to us. It was only after multiple hospitalizations, the bomb plot, a few suspensions for fighting, repeated skipping, and his very low GPA that Thomas's counseling office let us know that they could appoint a case manager to assist us with getting additional services in place. We didn't know that was an option, and we readily accepted. We needed all the help we could get.

The case manager's first priority was to figure out how to improve Thomas's overall school experience so that he can begin to engage in the learning process. The first step he wanted us to take was to request an evaluation for an Individualized Education Plan. We submitted a request through his guidance counselor to begin the process of determining if he met the criteria for an IEP. In the meantime, our case manager began visiting the school on a regular basis to check in with Thomas, but more often than not, when he would show up, no one would be able to locate him.

The case manager would call us to let us know what was happening while the school staff would fan out and search the building. This is when the administration finally started taking notice that Thomas was regularly missing, even though we had been speaking to them about his skipping for the past two years. We had assumed that he was remaining on the school premises most days, even though he was skipping his classes.

In prior years, he would sneak into the gymnasium or hang out in the restrooms until class was over. It seemed that now he was actually leaving the premises, and no one even noticed. Our case manager was very upset to say the least, and he started demanding that the school answer his questions about their security and safety protocols. The same questions we had been asking when we would try to find out where Thomas had been throughout the school day. His attendance records clearly show that he wasn't remaining in class.

Whenever we showed up at the school to speak to his guidance counselor or to the eighth grade principal, they would both refuse to speak with us. Not overtly, but they never seemed to be there whenever we were there. The secretary would tell us that they must have just stepped out of their offices; they were there a minute ago. They would be right back. I radioed them so it shouldn't be but a minute—on and on it went.

Those few minutes always turned into an hour or two until we would eventually be forced to leave. We spent weeks trying to track one of them down, to no avail. I didn't even know what either of them looked like to hunt them down myself. We continued to regularly meet with his teachers to talk about his progress or lack thereof, and his guidance counselor was required to attend those meetings as well, but she never showed up to any of them.

Our objective was to find out which classes he was skipping and how often, and if it was due to him not liking the teacher, not liking the subject, or something else. When was he leaving campus, and how was he leaving unnoticed? Where was he going? We couldn't help him, keep him safe, keep others safe, or break the cycle if we didn't have communication other than the automated messages. By then, the day was done, and it was too late for us to do anything about it.

After a few months, with his teachers' continued help, we were able to establish some sort of pattern. If Thomas stayed in the building in the mornings, he would inevitably sleep through the first class. If not, he walked right out the front door with none of the adults questioning him or stopping him. He would show back up around eleven, just in time for lunch. He would stay through both lunch periods and maybe go to his next class but then disappear again.

He would always show back up again, just in time to catch the afternoon bus home until he started the fire that suspended him for the remainder of the school year. Eventually, he would come walking through the front door around dinnertime and behave as though he had a perfectly normal day at school. We found that no matter what he was doing, he made sure he got to eat. I guess a growing boy has his priorities.

Thomas always seemed to have an appointment with someone, and whether we were going to the school to check him out for therapy, meet with his teachers, or try to catch his guidance counselor, we seemed to be there more than he was. After checking in with everyone and speaking to the police officers standing on the front steps, no one ever noticed his comings or goings. Our presence was often the only indication to the office staff that he was even missing.

After a building search was conducted, we would often go home to see if we could find him there. Sometimes he would be running out the back door while we were unlocking the front one. He would run outside so quickly that he would leave the TV and game system running. One time we tried to follow him in our car to see exactly where he was headed, but he was pretty good at sneaking through people's yards and hiding behind bushes, so we lost him pretty quickly.

If he managed to run out the back door with his shoes on, he would usually make it the three miles back to school, and then he would go to his current class and behave as though he had been there the whole time. If he ran out of the house without his shoes on, we figured out that he was climbing up onto the roof and hiding there until we would leave or the school day would end.

We've tried to convince him to come down many times, but he had a certain spot where he could lie down out of view and pretend that he wasn't there. We weren't about to climb up there ourselves to try to force him to come down. We would just go inside to wait him out. He has been known to sit on the black roof in the baking sun for over six hours. I'd rather just go to school myself.

He spent much more energy and effort sneaking than if he just sat in class. A few times, he came down from the roof and crawled up onto the front porch so that he could grab a pair of his shoes and escape. If we didn't stop him, he was convinced that he had fooled us, and we were none the wiser. With that much effort invested in being sneaky without being sneaky at all, we would usually let him go. Why not at this point? He had been caught, but he would never see it that way. He always seemed to think that he was able to slip one past us.

Christopher and I varied our schedules to be able to come home or stop by the school at random times throughout the week. We took the house key away from him to deter him from returning home to sleep or play video games, but then he just started breaking in and causing damage to the windows and the doors. Friends would call us to let us know whenever they saw him sitting under an overpass or walking down the street in the middle of the afternoon. We never knew where he would end up in a given day.

I called our police department to see if they offered any truancy assistance, and although their website said that they had a truancy department, I was assured that they did not offer that service to the community. The police officers at the middle school also told us that they couldn't help us once he was off the grounds, but they didn't seem to do anything to keep him on the grounds either.

Our days quickly turned into a cat and mouse chase. We had hoped that with him being caught again and again, he would realize that it would be better to just do what was right in the first place, but that realization never came. It wasn't long before we stopped running around after him because if we thwarted one plan, he just schemed up another one for the next day. It was exhausting, and every new scenario just stressed us out even more because we were absolutely powerless to change it. We resigned ourselves to the fact that no matter where he spent his days and no matter what he had gotten himself into, he would walk through the front door come dinnertime.

*****

The school was obviously not to blame for Thomas's choices, but we did feel like it was their responsibility to communicate with us and to enforce their own safety protocols that they claimed to already have in place. If they would have started working with us instead of against us and taken measures to assist us in keeping him safe and on the premises, I would not have had to contact the school board. After leaving dozens of messages and continually showing up at the school to speak with the principal or guidance counselor and being repeatedly avoided, to also having our IEP petition ignored, I had no choice but to go above them.

Once the school board was involved, the guidance counselor suddenly called me to set up an appointment. The first time I met with her, I asked to see Thomas's file. Certainly, after sixth and seventh grade, a few suspensions, a bomb plot, a bus fire, and him skipping over one hundred days of school the previous year, there had to be some information in his file. At the very least, my IEP request should be in there.

She went to pull his file to give to me, and when I opened it, there wasn't one piece on paper in it. She actually handed me an empty file with his name on it. I couldn't believe it. Where were his records? Where were all the papers I signed with each parent-teacher conference? Where was the information about his medication? Where was my IEP request? She couldn't say.

My husband and I went back to see her week after week. She knew she could no longer avoid us now that the school board was involved. She became more and more defensive and made more and more excuses with each visit. We had caught her in so many lies that we knew she couldn't be trusted. We asked if we could walk Thomas to his first period class in the mornings, hoping that he would then feel like he had to stay on-site, but we were told that parents were not allowed to be in the building. When we pressed to have someone at least watch the doors to make sure he didn't turn around and walk out within five minutes of us dropping him off, she surprisingly volunteered to wait for him each morning and walk him to his first-period class herself.

The next morning, she was there waiting, but the following day she was nowhere to be found. When we went back to find out if she was planning on keeping her commitment or if someone else on the security team could do it, she assured us that she would be waiting the following morning. Sure enough, she was there the next day, but never any of the following days. Back and forth this went, and it was clear that she, nor anyone else, really cared or really wanted to help us. As the days went by, we were treated with more and more hostility. They really didn't want to have to deal with us anymore, and they were giving our case manager just as much runaround.

One day we received a letter in the mail from the state's attorney's office. It was a threatening letter that said that they were going to press charges against us for not ensuring that our child attends school. It said that a court hearing would be scheduled if we did not ensure his attendance immediately. Before I had even finished reading the letter aloud, Christopher started dialing the state's attorney's office.

When he was connected to the assistant attorney, he introduced himself, explained the letter he was now holding in his hand, and then actually begged them to press charges. He assured them that they did not want to mess with him or hear what he had to say to the judge. The attorney stammered for a moment and then claimed it was only a warning notice and that it was nothing to be concerned about. I didn't know simple warning notices came with threats to prosecute. Thomas's lack of attendance was what we had been trying to get help with from the very start of the school year.

Shortly after that, we started getting phone calls from the school board asking us if we were going to sue them. They told us that we had a legal right to request a hearing and that we had a strong case against them. They told us that they had already lawyered up and had started preparing for us to file. We had no intention of suing them, but since they were already able to recognize that we had the right to take legal action, then why in the world were they not trying to remedy the situation? Taking them to court hadn't even crossed our minds. We just wanted them to do what they were supposed to do and to provide the services they were supposed to provide.

I found out that according to IDEA, Individuals with Disabilities Education Act's, procedural safeguards, schools must respond to a request for evaluation within a "reasonable time frame." Our state allows for no more than sixty school days to respond to a written request for an IEP evaluation. We were almost through the entire school year. We had to repeatedly go around the local school and contact the school board's ESE or Exceptional Student Education

Department that administers services for students with disabilities to get someone to speak with us.

I was on a first-name basis with much of their staff midway through the school year, and I had to repeatedly assure them that we were not seeking legal counsel. Maybe we should have, but we only asked that disciplinary action be taken in regard to the middle school's administrative neglect. We just wanted to get services in place for our child that they were legally required to provide. After relenting persistence, we finally signed his IEP at the end of May, eight months after the request was made and only two weeks before school was out.

*****

We were not surprised when we receive a notice in the mail that Thomas was being retained to repeat the eighth grade. Of course, he was. He hadn't attended the majority of the school year. His GPA had slipped to a 0.93, and that was with some of the teachers giving him a good grade for just showing up. We had no intention of him remaining at the same school for another year. Our experience with them was beyond terrible, and I'm sure they were as sick of dealing with us just as much as we were of them.

Christopher knew he was going to have to be very clear and forceful with his intention. He had lost all patience and respect for Thomas's principal months earlier. He found him cowardly, so he called and called and called until he was forced to pick up the phone and speak with him. The school had failed our family, and we knew another year wouldn't make a difference for Thomas. He wasn't going to suddenly change his behavior or start attending class, and the school was going to make absolutely no effort in helping us.

I had already begun exploring other school options. We could go the private-school route, knowing he would be kicked out in a matter of months because they wouldn't have to put up with his behavior. Until then, we would be paying a high tuition for him to maintain an empty seat. We could go a disciplinary route and send him to a locked-down school for troubled students, but our case manager actually advised us against that because Thomas would be exposed to things much worse than what he was already doing. There was an expectation on his part that Thomas would spiral out of control even more.

My mission was just to get Thomas into high school, and then the rest would be up to him. We couldn't make him learn, and we couldn't keep chasing him down either. If he ends up repeating ninth grade over and over again, maybe peer pressure or embarrassment would compel him to make better choices. I was simply trying to get him to the next step because things shift in high school. I needed him to be at a school that would be tougher on him and that would demand him to grow up a little and start taking responsibility for his actions. It was the difference between him being treated like a child and him being treated like a teenager growing into an adult.

Christopher made it very clear to the principal that day that it was not in his best interest to retain Thomas. If he did, he would be putting himself in a position to deal with our family for yet another year. He was also going to have to deal with Thomas, who had become a thorn in his side. My husband assured him that promoting Thomas was in everyone's best interests. The principal had said there was nothing he could do, but after that conversation, we received a revised report card in the mail that had been changed just enough to justify promoting Thomas to high school.

After I enrolled him in ninth grade, I received a call from the ESE Department. Unfortunately, they said Thomas could not be accepted to high school without passing prealgebra. Math was a specific area we targeted in his brand-new IEP because of his broad math skills, which included problem-solving and reasoning that had tested in the low range. His math calculation, which covers basic math skills (two-digit multiplication, regrouping, basic fractions, and so on) was also extremely low and could only be completed with much difficulty. He was completely unable to calculate change or analyze mathematical problems.

Basically, he had a limited fourth grade understanding. When I explained that to the ESE administrator, she suggested that I work with him virtually over the summer months to pass the course. She enrolled him in a prealgebra class and then sent me the links to get him started. All of us worked with him for weeks. His siblings tried to explain how to calculate slope and how to work a problem with fractions or exponents.

I took him to the office with me every day so that he could sit next to me and ask for help when he didn't understand an assignment. He would watch the tutorials over and over again and still not be able to comprehend what they were trying to teach him. It didn't matter how many times it was explained or how many times one of us would show him the steps; he just wasn't able to grasp any of it.

A thirty-minute minute lesson would turn into days. He would fail a quiz and then be required to review the whole lesson over again and take the quiz up to two more times only to get the same result. I was surprised that he actually tried really hard to complete the work. He wasn't happy to be made to do it, but I didn't encounter the same resistance we had witnessed with regular school attendance or even back when I homeschooled him. He seemed to want to get it done to move on to high school with his friend.

His course screen displayed big red Xs where he had failed his quizzes and tests. I wasn't the one struggling through it, and I found that very discouraging. Who decided giant red Xs on the home screen would be a positive motivator to keep trying? One day, I had decided that enough was enough. Do we put the mentally ill, paranoid child in a situation where he is confused, is being told he is failing at every attempt, and continue to force him to do what he is just not capable of doing? That combination is just begging for a violent outburst, a Baker Act, or a deep, depressive episode.

I called the school board back and told them that he would not be completing the course and that I felt it was ridiculous for them to demand that he complete it to advance to high school. He couldn't even get past the first module. They again told me that completing prealgebra was a requirement for all students, without exception. No matter what I said, I was getting nowhere.

Math exceptions were in his IEP. Why do you think we fought so hard to get him those exceptions? He legitimately needed them. I asked if he could be enrolled in a remedial math class instead, but she said that the high schools in our district did not offer basic math classes. I was so frustrated with arguing with them that I asked my husband to call them to see if he could make any further progress.

When he called back to plead our case one more time, he asked the administrator if there was anything else that could be done for our son. He asked her if she would expect a child in the fourth grade to complete prealgebra. She said that would not be reasonable, and they would never expect that of a child in the fourth grade. So Christopher responded by stating that our son has been tested with having a math understanding of only a fourth grader. She was quick to express her condolences for that, but Thomas was going to have to complete prealgebra to enter high school.

He asked her again if she would expect a fourth grader to be able to pass prealgebra. She again responded that it would not be reasonable to put that expectation on a fourth grader. So he repeated again that Thomas only had a fourth grade understanding of mathematics. She again apologized for that but followed it up by stating that Thomas would have to complete prealgebra to advance to ninth grade. Round and round they went, repeating the same dialogue back and forth for almost five minutes. He actually timed it. There was an obvious disconnect and lack of basic logic in play.

We continued to press the issue as far up the chain of command as we could go. Whenever I hit a roadblock or my calls were not being answered, our case manager stepped in. He knew everyone by name and exactly whom to contact. He was even more aggressive than we were—to the point that they contacted his supervisor and demanded that he cease and desist. Thankfully, as parents, they couldn't stop us from calling so we continued in our efforts. What other choice did we have? We couldn't just leave him in limbo, learning nothing and going nowhere.

I imagine that they saw our phone number on their caller ID and groaned. Trust me. I was just as sick of calling them as they probably were with dealing with me. When I was in high school, I remember there being classes for students who couldn't pass higher math. My husband actually helped tutor in a remedial math class for one of his teachers. I couldn't understand why our district didn't offer something like that. What do the other students like Thomas do? He couldn't possibly be the only one in the whole district who struggles to grasp mathematical concepts.

Because of our relentless insistence, they did end up making an exception by allowing us to enroll him in high school just a few days before the new school year began. However, he was placed in a standard algebra class just as if he had completed the prealgebra course. I was told that he would continue to take the required algebra class throughout high school until he passed it just like everyone else, regardless of any delays or gaps in his understanding. His IEP would make sure that as long as he tried, he would receive a passing grade.

We knew that he would never understand anything he was being taught. It is impossible to do algebra when you don't know your multiplication table or how to divide and work fractions. I told the ESE administrator that basically my son will never be taught what he really needs to learn. There was silence on the other end of the phone. I guess there was nothing more to say.

CHAPTER 13

Submit yourselves therefore to God.
Resist the devil, and he will flee from you.
—James 4:7

It may sound odd, but whenever I have struggled with being angry with Thomas, I have reminded myself of Moses and his many difficulties with the Israelites in the Old Testament. Through Moses, they found their freedom and witnessed amazing miracles, but they still grumbled and rebelled against him and God every step of the way—so much so that, as a punishment, that whole generation didn't see the promises of God fulfilled in their lifetime.

In Numbers 16:21, Korah who was the great-grandson of Levi the priest, led a revolt against his cousins, Moses and Aaron. He disagreed with their leadership, and along with his accomplices, Dathan and Abiram, he gathered a following of 250 men who were respected members of the council, and together they led a revolt. Of course, this angered God. The Israelites had been grumbling against the Lord for years.

God became so angry with them that He caused the ground to split open and swallow up Korah, Dathan, and Abiram, along with their wives and children and all their possessions. The earth closed over them, and in an instant, they were gone. Then fire came out from God and burned up the remaining men who had followed Korah. Nothing was left but the charred remains of hundreds of men.

When I read biblical accounts like this, it reminds me that even God gets angry with the rebelliousness of His children. There are a few times in scripture where He wants to destroy them and simply start over. The Israelites just wouldn't listen and trust that He was taking care of them. Of course, there is grace and mercy now, and I have never wanted to destroy Thomas, but I have been so angry with him that I just didn't want to deal with him any longer. In some way, Old Testament stories like this one have assured me that I'm not crazy for being angry with my kid. If even God experiences anger, it is okay when I feel angry too. What I do with my anger is what matters.

Ephesians 4:26–27 says, "In your anger do not sin. Do not let the sun go down while you are still angry, and do not give the devil a foothold." I have always had to find a place of compassion and forgiveness toward Thomas, which hasn't been easy. I have tried my best to guard my heart from becoming bitter and resentful. I recognize that my anger really comes from a place of hurt. I know that hurting people like Thomas hurt other people. He knows no other way to be. Working through my anger and recognizing my need to forgive him from one event to the next has been an ongoing struggle.

There have been countless nights where my husband and I have lain in bed together discussing the latest difficulty we were facing. There were so many unanswered questions that I wish I could sit face-to-face with God and get some direct answers. Whenever I would ask Him why He had asked us to adopt Thomas in the first place, knowing we were going to have to struggle and fight every step of the way, I never once heard an answer. I never felt like God was punishing us or anything like that. I can't say that I've ever been angry with God. I've just struggled with understanding His plan and purpose in it all.

Christopher has found solace in believing that adopting Thomas wasn't really about us at all but rather about him. He feels that we had been asked to lay our lives down for Thomas in hopes that he would find wholeness and freedom. I have found that by making the choice to sacrifice what I want has helped me understand Christ in a deeper way. Jesus didn't want to be beaten and crucified, but He knew that by laying down His will, humanity could find freedom.

It is only through His example that my husband and I have been able to continually choose to love and care for Thomas through the years. Our sacrifice doesn't begin to compare with Jesus, who sacrificed everything even to death, but just the day-to-day reality of what it takes to put someone else's needs above your own and then to be rejected by the one you are trying to save has made me appreciate what Christ has done all the more.

I only wish that I had the same ability as Jesus had to immediately identify the cause of what we were dealing with. He always knew when someone was in sin had a demon or when they were bound by iniquity. With Thomas, we have struggled to identify what it was that we were fighting against. Christopher and I have pondered the differences between nature verses nurture. We have wrestled over how much of what we were dealing with was actually the demonic versus a physical illness or a chemical imbalance.

Whenever I have felt strongly that we were dealing with the demonic, my husband would be sure that we were reaping behaviors stemming from his chemical imbalance. If I felt something was rooted in generational iniquity, he would feel like he was just responding out of his brokenness and the protective way he had learned to survive. Back and forth, our discussions would go. Whenever I would be convinced that what I was perceiving was correct, something would happen that would make me question everything all over again.

Our conversations would often end with a tiresome and weary, "I don't know." Everything seemed muddled and clouded. There was so much more at work than what we could see on the surface. We were usually so preoccupied with dealing with the latest crisis that the struggle to get to the root of things was often just too draining. It had gotten to the point that we were just happy to have survived a day without a major meltdown or altercation.

With the whole family in a state of trauma, I spent so many late nights checking in with the other children and making sure they were okay. Of course, no one in the family was actually okay. We had started to retreat more and more into our bedrooms, living separate and isolated lives from one another. Everyone was interacting with Thomas as little as possible and spending more and more of their time behind closed doors.

It became easier to let Thomas have the living space to play his video games than to have him wandering around restless or stirring up trouble. At least when he played video games, he was home and safe, and his attention was focused on the game and not on any of us. Unfortunately, those brief moments of peace meant sacrificing our communal living space, which separated the rest of us from one another even more. It was only when he was out of the house that we would all come out of hiding and really spend time together.

Our family had become a shadow of what it once was. Our home use to overflow with friends and be full of laughter. We used to live in a flurry of activity with lots of game nights, outings, and parties. Now our friends were far away, and our home was crippled in silence and suffering. The loneliness and isolation we felt was difficult to bear at times. Our older children lamented the days of our past and longed for change. They themselves kept busy outside of the home as much as possible to escape our daily reality. We had become the complete opposite of what we were only a few years before. Things had changed so quickly.

Over time, the answers to our many questions about Thomas settled on yes. Yes, we were dealing with the demonic. Yes, we were dealing with illness and chemical imbalance; and yes, we were dealing with a wounded soul with generational iniquity. We were fighting a war on all fronts, and every aspect was at play in every battle we had faced. We couldn't gain ground in one area without another one taking over.

All the way back in the Garden of Eden, the devil came to deceive and destroy the perfect union between creation and Creator. With his deception being received and then acted upon, death entered the world. Sickness infected creation and corrupted it. With this first act of sin, death and disease gained access to creation. Now illness and disease are a normal part of our existence, and none of us know a world uncorrupted by it.

Generation after generation, sin has been passed down from parent to child. Exodus 34:6–7 says,

> The Lord, the Lord, the compassionate and gracious God, slow to anger, abounding in love and faithfulness, maintaining love to thousands, and

> forgiving wickedness, rebellion and sin. Yet he does not leave the guilty unpunished; he punishes the children and their children for the sin of the parents to the third and fourth generation.

We all carry iniquity passed down through our family lines, but iniquity can be removed through repentance. I believe many of us are unaware of how iniquity can affect our daily lives. We have all heard someone say something like, "She acts just like her mother." How about, "My father was a drunk, and his father was a drunk before him"? These are examples of iniquities passed down from one generation to the next. I'm sure we have all seen patterns in our own families, both positive and negative. Curses and blessings are both passed generationally.

The demonic comes into play when we dig deep, down to the root of all things operating in contrast to God. God is good. He is love, joy, laughter, and peace. He is truth and wisdom. He is gentle and powerful. He is ever patient and merciful. He is always faithful. The devil is pain and suffering. He is pride and arrogance, rebellion and anger. He is full of deceit. There is no truth in him, and according to John 10:10, he is a thief and a liar, and he comes only to kill, steal, and destroy.

I believe the devil takes full advantage of our wounded places. If he can break us and destroy our hopes and dreams, then we will be unable to step into our true identity and purpose in Christ. He fills those wounded places with shame, rejection, and pain. He speaks lies to our minds that encourage us to pick up false beliefs about ourselves and others. Through our brokenness, we can then speak curses and make vows against those who have hurt us, which binds us and traps us in sin.

We witnessed a vow in action when we pulled our car away from the foster home, and at three years old, Thomas defiantly started counting in the back seat. The foster mother had just told him that he was stupid and that he didn't even know his numbers or how to count. He started counting and clearly intended to prove her wrong. Even in his little three-year-old mind, he had already made a vow of, "I'll show her." More than ten years later, if you even hint to Thomas that he doesn't know something, he becomes instantly offended and angry.

Scripture talks a lot about renewing our minds, keeping our minds set on the things of the Lord, and repenting, which simply means to change our minds about something. Our mind can be a powerful thing. If you view yourself as a victim, then everything you do, every decision you make, will be filtered through the belief that you are a victim. People will actually victimize you further. If you absolutely believe you cannot do something, then you probably never will. Especially if you made up your mind before you even give it a try.

If you believe there is no way anyone could possibly love you, then you will struggle to recognize love when it is given, and you will go through life pushing away everyone around you who does. Just the opposite is also true. If you choose to believe you are worthy of love, then you will be able to give and receive love more freely, recognizing the counterfeit and embracing the purest form itself. We manifest that which we believe.

Therefore, one of our greatest strengths and one of our greatest hindrances to ourselves is our own personal belief system. What we believe about ourselves determines how we think and what we can achieve. If you embrace your fate in that your father was poor, his father was poor, and his father before him was poor, then you are less likely to break that systemic cycle that has become a generational curse in your family.

Sometimes things are spoken over us when we are very young like in Thomas's experience, and we have taken them on as part of our identity. For instance, if you have a critical parent who tells you that you're stupid and you will never grow up to amount to anything and you'll be just like _____ (fill in the blank with the one person who has disappointed or hurt them the most), then you can grow up carrying that belief with you into adulthood.

It can become so ingrained in who you are that you don't even realize it. It can permeate every aspect of your life where you might think, "Why would I even try to go to college? I'm not smart enough to do that." On the flip side, what if you grew up being told that you are smart and that you could achieve your dreams and you actually believe that? How far would that mind-set take you?

Sometimes beliefs are born out of what is modeled around us or what we infer out of our experiences and the experiences of others in our lives. They can be made on a deep, subconscious level, which can result in vows being made in response to them, such as, "My father walked out on my mother, and it caused us to struggle, so I will make sure that I will never be dependent upon a man." How about, "My family abandoned me. I don't need them. I don't need anyone. I will show them that I can make it on my own." In the case of many adoptive children, they see that they have been abandoned by their birth parents; and no matter the cause, they can feel unworthy, unlovable, and not valued. After all, they weren't good enough to be kept in the first place.

Even if they were given up for adoption with the most self-less and purest of good intentions, they can still feel abandoned. Many people have coined it the "spirit of adoption," and the spirit of adoption can be good or bad. It all depends upon your mind-set. As Christians, we are taught that we have the spirit of adoption, having been accepted as children into the family of God. That is a wonderful and beautiful identity to embrace.

An adopted child could choose to see that their new family specifically selected them over all the other children that they could have chosen and that the adoptive family set out to provide them with a loving home that, for whatever reason, their birth parents were unable or unwilling to provide. They could view themselves as being special and unique with the blessing of growing up in a better situation, or they could choose to see it as they were only adopted by their new family because they were abandoned and discarded by their birth family. If they choose the negative aspect, then their childhood will probably be tainted with feelings of being different and rejected instead being able to receive the gift of acceptance and adoption.

Sometimes not knowing the whole truth works against them because we as humans tend to go to the worst-case scenario, and the devil is a liar and a thief who takes full advantage of every opportunity to work against us. Scripture tells us in Philippians 4:8 to "think on whatever is true, whatever is noble, whatever is right, whatever is pure, whatever is lovely, whatever is admirable. If anything is praiseworthy, think about such things and the God of Peace will be with you."

Why would it tell us that? There is a release in the spirit for those things. Just as there are demons for hate, anger, strife, malice, envy, and jealousy, there are also angels for things like freedom, joy, peace, and laughter. If we allow God to minister healing and wholeness with a renewing of our minds, there can be a manifestation of the work of the Holy Spirit in our lives that produces the fruits of the Spirit, which is love, joy, peace, patience, kindness, goodness, faithfulness, gentleness, and self-control.

I have been able to see the natural and the spiritual, the soul hurts and the generational iniquities, the vows and a negative mindset all at work within Thomas. He has all the natural effects of neglect, abuse, and feelings of abandonment that created great insecurity and fear within him. Through his natural fear, a spirit of fear was given place and authority to act in his life. He probably doesn't remember a time when fear wasn't present.

As Thomas was developing and growing as a small boy, his body responded to his neglect and abuse, and hypervigilance and chemical malfunction developed, which altered his brain function. Since he was placed with a caregiver who spoke curses over him, he took on the belief that he wasn't lovable, he wasn't going to amount to anything, and that he wasn't important or valuable to anyone—plus many, many more. I believe the devil continues to speak those lies over him to this day.

The layers and layers of wounding he has experienced, no one has been able to fully unravel. We don't know all of the ways that the verbal and physical abuse has affected his soul. Then top that off with deep sorrow and depression, and his negative feelings toward adoption and all the struggles that can bring about with identity and self-worth. Then you add in the spiritual component with all the lies and deceptions and twisting of the truth, and you end up with one big convoluted mess.

The only one who really knows how to bring wholeness to Thomas is God. He knows when each and every wound was inflicted and the offshoots that twisted out of each place of pain. He knows Thomas better than Thomas knows himself. I know He wants to heal him, but Thomas has to open his heart up to God, which he has refused to do. Thomas really struggles with the concept that there is a God out there who loves him. He doesn't believe that he is worthy of love, but I have seen the Holy Spirit speak to him. I've watched as Thomas has put his fingers in his ears in effort to block out His voice.

*****

Late one evening, I was home with our children while my husband was away traveling. I had noticed that the atmosphere in our home had become very negative and that the children seemed more on edge than usual. Everyone was becoming easily frustrated with one another, and name-calling and eye-rolling had infused its way into their daily interactions. I gathered the kids in the living room to talk about what I had been seeing and to have everyone share what was really going on. Usually these family meetings were done when everyone was present, but with my husband away for a few weeks, I knew it couldn't wait.

I helped each of them express their frustrations and struggles and then led them into a time of repentance and asking for forgiveness from one another. As the older ones opened up, the conversation shifted into a time of encouragement and prayer. This night didn't start out any differently than many of the other times we have had to stop and clear the air. With a house full of teenagers and our constant challenges with Thomas, there always seemed to be something that needed to be discussed or arguments that needed to be mediated.

Since my husband and I have always fostered an environment where feelings could be openly expressed, these times could have both extremes from fierce confrontation and yelling to someone weeping with a pile of tissues in their lap. These family-meeting times have relieved a lot of tension in the home over the years, and they have served to repair a lot of damage and misunderstandings between the different relationships.

The five of us had been spending a lot of time at our church. A friend of ours had been going there in the evenings to worship and teach voice lessons. She started hearing footsteps and doors slamming when she was the only one in the building. She started feeling very uneasy about being there alone, so she asked a small group of us to come pray and worship with her. One evening turned into two weeks. We went throughout the whole building praying and worshiping together, and we encountered the spirit realm in a very real and powerful way.

Spiritual discernment is a prominent gifting in my family, so seeing and identifying spiritual activity comes pretty naturally for us. Some of us see into the spirit realm as clearly as they see the physical world, interacting with angels and demons regularly. Some of us can hear angels and demons, speaking to them either in English or in an angelic or demonic tongue. We can feel and sense them in the atmosphere, and we have had some powerful encounters whenever we have gathered together and really pressed into the spirit.

I can only assume that our time worshiping and praying together had made us sensitive to the things of the spirit realm that evening while we met to work through some family dynamics. One of the main reasons I called everyone together was to address the mocking and disrespect I had been witnessing. We had spent all of this time praising God through the church, but the kids couldn't manage to be kind and respectful of one another once we got home. I set out to uproot the cause, and that was when our eyes were opened to see the spirit of mockery standing in the living room with us. It was the spiritual result of all the nastiness that had been coming from their lips for weeks.

Each of them spent time repenting for using mockery as a weapon against each other, and one by one they broke agreement with it and told it to go. Mockery was dressed in a nice pinstriped suit and tie. He held a thin microphone in his hand like a daytime-game-show host. He had a booming announcer voice that he used to mock each of them until they all told him he had to go. Once the agreement was broken, he left very disappointed that he had been ousted. After he was gone, we were pondering what we had just witnessed when we caught a glimpse of something else moving in the shadows of another room.

It seemed like God was making a way for us to deal with things in the spirit realm that evening that we had been unable to see before. We spent a few hours going from room to room and dealing with whatever He revealed to us. We found spirits attached to unforgiveness, insecurity, addiction, pride, wounds from past betrayals, and even insomnia. The reason why I am sharing this event is because of what happened next.

Thomas's bedroom was the last room we went into that night. As we stepped into his room, we counted six demons huddled together on his bed and another one standing outside, peering through the bedroom window. They were nervous and were trying their best to hide from us. One by one, we identified them as Suicide, Overdose, Addiction, Rage, Abandonment, Loneliness, and Cat. All of them made sense to me except Cat. What in the world did Cat mean? We told it to explain its name. It refused to answer at first, but after some pressing, it said that it was Cat as in "cat got your tongue."

All the times I have struggled to get Thomas to answer me suddenly made sense. Cat had been literally—well, spiritually—holding his tongue. There have been so many times, especially when he was younger, that you could clearly see he was struggling with wanting to say something, but he couldn't get the words out. Silent tears would roll down his cheeks, but he always remained silent. Even as I started to explain to Thomas how he could get rid of all of those spirits that evening, he couldn't speak to me. He would start to move his mouth, but no sound would come out.

I had long suspected that Thomas was manifesting a demon. There had been no other explanation for the way his body would change and the rage he would exude. He had been manifesting before he ever came to live with us. I clearly identified Rage from the very start. I knew the voices he was hearing were also demons, but I never suspected he had seven in total. Rage was the only one that I had clearly seen take over his body. I had been able to silence the voices from time to time, but I was never able to get rid of them. Maybe I was, and they were simply coming back.

Those demons belong to Thomas. Whether he knowingly invited them in or they found entry through his wounded places, they had become a part of him, and they had been given authority to remain. Thomas was thirteen at this time, and I believe many of the demons had been with him since he was a very small child. It seemed that only he had the authority to truly send them away. I knew that until he faced them and dealt with the root of their connection, or God supernaturally delivers him, those demons would remain.

We stood in a circle and joined hands in the middle of his bedroom. I started by asking Thomas if he believed in God, and after a moment of contemplation, he shook his head yes. Then I asked him if he believed that Jesus came to die for him, and he again shook his head yes. I told him that if he believed, he needed to confess it with his mouth, and he needed to say it out loud. After a few attempts, and with much struggle and effort, he was able to whisper it. He tried again and again until Cat's grip loosened enough for him to speak clearly. Then one by one, I told him how to send each and every demon away.

They didn't just leave as soon as he told them too. It took time for him to speak with authority. His little body trembled as they resisted and struggled to maintain their grip on him. Eventually, each one left, some slinking out the window and others running away into the night. By the time they were all gone, Thomas was smiling and laughing freely, something I had never seen him do before.

Exhausted and weary, we all went to bed, but not until we spent some time explaining to Thomas that each of those demons would try to return again. The four of us explained in detail how he alone had the authority and strength to resist them and to send them away again at any time. We assured him that we were standing with him and would help him any time he was struggling. He said he understood, and I prayed his mind and spirit were clear enough to comprehend what we were saying.

I lay in bed that night pondering all that had happened and for the first time, truly hopeful that Thomas had finally found his freedom. It was such a surreal experience. I was only sorry my husband had missed it. How in the world could I adequately explain to him what had happened that evening? It was crazy and surreal, and I could hardly wrap my brain around it all myself. It was a completely supernatural God experience that I knew I could never fully explain with words. It was one encounter I will never ever forget.

The next day was a complete turnaround from the days before. There was a renewed peace resting in the house again. Later that day, as we sat around the dinner table, Thomas laughed and joked right along with everyone else, and he had a new ease about him. It was amazing to see. The other kids and I kept looking at one another in bewilderment. He was a completely different person. There was a twinkle in his eye we had never seen before.

I couldn't wait for my husband to come home to see the change in Thomas that we were seeing. The rest of us kept a careful watch over him and his behavior, looking for any evidence that the demons were trying to return. We checked in with him repeatedly, and he maintained that he felt good; but after a few days, we could see him slowly slipping back into silence. His head was dropping lower and lower, and he started avoiding eye contact with us again.

By the end of a week, the twinkle was gone from his eyes, and his laughter had ceased. His gaze had turned downward toward the floor, and he had closed himself off from us again. Every time we pursued the conversation of what had happened and that we could tell the demons to go away again, he got squirmy and agitated. He rejected any conversation about it. He started telling us that what we had experienced didn't really happen. We were making it all up. Everything was a lie. Then he was gone. Christopher returned home to the same Thomas he had always known. He never got to see the brief transformation. He has never seen him truly free as the rest of us had.

A few weeks later in a moment of transparency, Christopher asked Thomas why he had let the demons come back. Thomas said that he was too lonely without them and that he just didn't know how to live separate from them and their ever-present voices. He chose bondage over freedom. Freedom was unknown and scary.

Freedom felt different. Freedom didn't come with the same restraints and chains that he had known his whole life. Going back to what was comfortable was the easier choice.

From that moment forward, he was under their influence more than ever before. Six of the seven demons had returned, and new ones had been added to their number. From Suicide came Sadness and Depression. From Abandonment came Paranoia. From Rage came Anger and Rebellion. Overdose never returned, but Schizophrenia took its place. He started with seven and now had twelve demons in all.

Each of the spirits continually fought with one another to gain control over him. Abandonment holds him by the right arm, and Rage holds him by the left. They yank him to and fro resulting in severe mood swings from one extreme to the other. When Abandonment has control, he is overwhelmed with Sadness and Depression and struggles with Suicide and Paranoia. When Rage has control, he becomes manic with Anger and Rebelliousness and is driven to do bad things. Cat rests on his head once again, holding his tongue in silence.

CHAPTER 14

God is our refuge and strength
an ever-present help in trouble.
—Proverbs 46:1

I have always dreaded going to the counseling office and having to attend family therapy sessions, but therapy is part of the process when you are raising a child with mental health issues. There's just no way around it. If I felt that therapy was actually making a difference for Thomas or for our family, I would be all in, but we have never seen any real or long-lasting benefits from him going week after week, year after year.

We've had many therapists—two or three we've really liked—but most of them we didn't care for or feel that they were adequately equipped or educated enough to deal with the severity of Thomas's diagnosis. We were surprised to learn that many of them didn't know what reactive attachment disorder was, and if they had heard of it, that was only because they had recently attended a seminar overviewing the disorder but then admitted that they had never worked with an RAD patient before.

Why we repeatedly got assigned therapists that didn't understand RAD was beyond me. The longer we have walked through this process, the more we have realized that not knowing was more common than knowing. I guess this is attributed to how recent this disorder has been researched and identified. There have been many times where we have had to explain what RAD is and then ask the therapist to please research it in hopes that their understanding of the disorder would assist them in developing an effective treatment plan.

I have no idea if any of them took that initiative. We have never had a therapist speak to us about any RAD identifiers that they were working through or may have noticed while speaking with Thomas. His treatment plans have always been focused on his outward behavior and how they could help him control his anger. Sessions focused on teaching him to count whenever he became angry and to walk away whenever he wanted to lash out—beneficial coping skills, but they were superficial to what was making him angry in the first place.

His therapist in fourth and fifth grade was the only one who had been able to dig deep and get Thomas to open up about his struggles and his pain. As Thomas got older, he was more resistant to expressing anything other than his current frustrations with school and peer relationships. His therapy sessions usually consisted of him complaining about what this person or that person had done to him that week. There was a protective barrier he had placed around the deepest parts of himself that he did not let anyone else come near. It seemed that most of his therapists failed to notice that it was even there.

To really help Thomas, you have to understand the lack of attachment and bonding that he has with other people. You have to understand his deep trauma and fear. His level of fear goes extremely deep and is ingrained in the very fabric of who he is. You must also recognize how the spirit realm has taken advantage of his brokenness. Every aspect has affected how Thomas views himself and what he believes about the other people around him. Looking at his whole person and understanding these broken areas deep within him will completely alter a therapeutic approach. It would take the focus off his outward behavior and cause you to go deep to the foundational wounds that he carries. Otherwise, you are trying to treat all the behaviors on the surface that are just by-products of a deeply wounded child.

Whenever we've been assigned a new therapist, those first few months are draining and difficult for Christopher and me. The appointments always begin with one-on-one sessions between Thomas and the therapist in order for them to get to know each other and start building a rapport. That is very important. The downside of that for us specifically is that Thomas has plenty of time to paint a particular picture of who we are and our relationship with him. He is such a good manipulator, and for a few weeks, he has a captive audience.

He has a way of playing the victim that seems to get therapists to believe whatever he tells them. He was a victim. He was treated horribly, but Thomas doesn't separate between then and now. You would think that with years of training and with the type of clientele these therapists can see, there would be some hesitation at taking a mentally ill child completely at their word. They are provided with his file. They shouldn't be completely unaware or unprepared.

I have been surprised over and over again at how often they believe whatever he has told them. It can take us months to discover and unravel the things that he has said. Knowing that instantly puts my husband and me in a defensive position from the start. We have had to approach every family session with great caution, knowing that every gesture, every glance, every word is being used to corroborate what Thomas has already told them.

I feel that child therapists, at least most of the ones we have encountered, approach families with a preconceived assumption that all of the child's problems stem from a lack of parenting or some other type of dysfunction within the family. I concede that that might be the case in many situations, maybe even most. However, I don't think that should be an automatic given when taking on a new client, at least not with families like ours who have adopted.

I would think that all children who have come from foster care have at least some degree of trauma, loss, and anger that needs to be worked through. That doesn't mean it was inflicted by the adoptive family. I have rarely felt that we were approached with an open mind and a willingness to assess our family dynamics without prior bias. Most of his therapists have been shocked to discover that Thomas lives with an intact family where the parents are not divorced, not on drugs, and are consistently employed and present in his life.

It has usually taken about six months for a new therapist to figure out that we're not exactly who Thomas says that we are. He paints us as being horrible parents who are cruel and abusive, and he claims that his siblings treat him terribly. He had one particular therapist convinced that we completely ignore him and exclude him from all of our family activities, even holidays and birthdays. He has also claimed that we don't care or provide for him in any way—probably because I wouldn't take him shoe shopping at the mall that week.

One therapist accidentally gave us some of her session notes, and after weeks and weeks of individual and family sessions, she wrote that she had come to the same conclusion as Thomas. She believed we were actually excluding him and not allowing him to participate in any family activities when, in reality, he was excluding himself and choosing to remain isolated from us. We thought that we were making some headway and starting to turn her attention away from us and onto Thomas, but apparently not.

Thomas needed some real emotional and mental support because he wasn't able to open up to either one of us, and he had spent years stuffing everything he was feeling deep down inside of himself. It wasn't doing Thomas any good to meet with a therapist week after week to end up not even scratching the surface. It was infuriating to watch the twisted lies that came out of his mouth being accepted as truth. If it wasn't a requirement for me to attend these sessions, I wouldn't have. I dreaded just about every minute of the whole process.

The one thing that ultimately works to our advantage is that Thomas is a very cyclical being. He follows the same pattern year after year. Christopher was the first to notice the pattern, and it has been a huge help for us in recognizing Thomas's downward spirals. We have tried to explain it to his therapists and psychiatrists many times in hopes that they could assist him with an alternative voice of reason and ultimately provide him with some positive coping skills. At the very least, an avenue for him to talk about what he is feeling.

You see, Thomas is the easiest to deal with during the summer months, mostly due to the fact that it is the one time of the year that the least is required of him. He doesn't have to get up each morning for school. He has more personal free time, and he doesn't have a bunch of adults telling him what he can and cannot do every day.

Come August, he begrudgingly starts school. Everything is relatively calm at first, and his new teachers usually think we're crazy when we set up our initial meeting with them. They just can't believe what we're saying because Thomas is good at keeping quiet and avoiding attention in new situations.

He starts slipping mentally by the end of September, and by the beginning to middle of October, he will end up being admitted into a psychiatric facility without fail. After two days or so, Thomas will assure the doctors that he no longer wants to harm himself or anyone else. They end up discharging him because he "promises not to do anything," therefore satisfying the need for them to retain him any longer. We found it quite shocking that an unstable person could make a simple promise and be considered safe all of a sudden. I mean, he keeps threatening to murder his family in their sleep, but as long as he has promised not to, then I guess it's okay.

His brief stay in a facility does offer him a moment to mentally reset himself, and his medication is usually adjusted during that time. Once he's back home, he does his best to hold himself together for a week or two so that he doesn't give us a reason to send him away again. During this period of time, he is the most attentive and polite child who goes above and beyond with anything we ask of him. It's actually quite creepy and abnormal, but it isn't long before he settles back into a normal routine again.

He barely makes it through to his winter break, and Christmas is a great distraction for him as he is determined to be on his best behavior so that he can get some good gifts out of us. January rolls around, and he returns to school and seems to make a marginal effort for the first week or so. He begins to slip deeper and deeper toward depression through February, and by the beginning to mid-March, he ends up being Baker Acted again. Repeat the same scenario as before, and he is back home and back in school before you know it—as back in school as he ever really is with maintaining an even lower GPA of 0.47.

Some of his teachers have contacted us by this time to apologize for not believing us at the beginning of the school year. We find their apologies both validating and infuriating, but we press on and barely survive to the end of the school year. Thomas is quite done with everything surrounding it by then. Now we are back to summer break where he is at his best. We got to the point where we could anticipate his mental breakdowns like clockwork. Whenever we would see him start to spiral out of control, we would have to stop and think about where we were in the year, and it always lined up with this repetitive pattern.

The only thing about that is that we were the only ones who could see it coming, and where we live, you can't get preemptive help within the mental health community. We couldn't get a medicine change just because we believed he was about to go off the rails. We couldn't preemptively admit him to a psych facility without there being a direct cause. Our only option was to wait until all hell broke loose. Then we were in a place to get some temporary assistance, even if it was only for a couple of days. By that point, we just needed a break for our own well-being, and we welcomed any amount of time away from him where we knew he would be safely contained.

*****

Traveling of any kind was usually out of the question for me, even though my husband and I were missionaries and traveling was a necessary part of our ministry. Balancing our ministry needs with the needs of the family was growing increasingly difficult with the demands of Thomas's care, combined with the everyday needs of our other three children, who were learning to drive, going to prom, and heading off to college. My husband usually traveled without me, and from time to time, our older children traveled with him.

Whenever we have insisted that Thomas go with us somewhere like a restaurant, he would eat in silence and then pace and fidget and repeatedly ask if he could go to the car or go outside to wander the parking lot—anything to get away from the family. He pretty much made our time out together uncomfortable, so much so that we would often return home earlier than planned so that we wouldn't have to deal with the way he was acting any longer than necessary.

Eventually, we started letting Thomas remain at home. Whenever we gave him the choice, he always opted to stay behind. No amount of entertainment enticed him to spend time with us. When we would come back home, it would be evident that he was resentful that we had gone somewhere without him and had a nice evening together. He could have joined us, but he only did when forced. Without fail, we would find out in our next family therapy session that Thomas had claimed that we had excluded him and refused to let him go.

He was so deceived by the demonic spirits that were working against him that his reality was twisted and skewed. I started noticing just how agitated and uncomfortable he was whenever we were around him. Of course, RAD factors into that, but I started seeing it from a spiritual perspective. His demons hated the Holy Spirit within us and the angelic atmosphere of our home. I could feel a shift in the atmosphere every time Thomas crossed the threshold. At times, the demonic presence he carries with him would be so strong that it would literally make me nauseous.

They are constantly speaking lies in his ears. They have been telling him that we hate him and that we wish he would kill himself or run away for years now. I could see Thomas struggling under the weight of their relentless voices and his feelings of loneliness and isolation that they were magnifying. Deep down, Thomas desperately longs to be accepted and loved and to be a part of a family, but he has allowed those voices to convince him that we don't want him and that his life is worthless. I can't even begin to imagine what living in that reality would feel like.

With his unpredictable behavior and the increasing spiritual tension, we knew that traveling overseas with Thomas would be tricky. If he couldn't stand to spend an hour with us out in public and he did everything he could to avoid us, how in the world could we begin to manage him in an unknown environment thousands of miles from home? I was relieved when he said he wasn't interested in going on a mission with his father like the others had done. I didn't want the mission hindered or his siblings' travel opportunities to become a source of further resentment for him.

Working out our travel schedule was still a challenge with needing to determine who would go and who would stay behind. With relocating, we no longer had a support network in place to assist us in any way. Our friends and families were too far away. Our children had no grandparents, aunts, or uncles around, and establishing new relationships had been difficult for us. Although our oldest was an adult by this time, bearing the weight and responsibility of Thomas's care was too great of a burden for him, and we used him sparingly: partly because Thomas doesn't listen to anything he tells him to do, so fighting is inevitable.

Getting away and taking some time alone together with just the two of us was nearly impossible. It had been years since my husband and I attempted anything more than dinner and a movie. As long as one parent was home or he knew we were nearby, Thomas was relatively restrained and didn't cause too much trouble. Being gone over a longer period of time just gave Thomas unsupervised opportunity to misbehave. There was a definite uptick whenever dad was away, but as long as I was there, I could usually manage.

When Thomas was fourteen years old, I received a call from my father letting me know that my grandmother had died. I was determined to not miss her funeral, so my husband and I made plans to travel back to our hometown to attend. When we moved away, we left behind some heirloom furniture that had been passed down to our daughter from her paternal grandmother. It had been sitting in storage for years now, and we decided to take advantage of the journey to bring it back with us.

It was going to be a quick turnaround trip of four days so that we didn't leave Thomas at home for too many days without us. Leaving the other two wouldn't be a problem (our oldest son was living on his university's campus), but adding Thomas to the mix made the situation unpredictable. We gave him permission to spend the weekend with his neighbor friend in hopes of keeping him occupied and out of the house. Thomas had seemed to be doing okay, and I was determined to not miss my grandmother's funeral. I had sacrificed so many other things to remain at home with him. This was not going to be one of them.

We were only a few hours away when my husband's phone rang. On the other end of the line was our son Isaiah, who seemed quite shaken. The police were at our home handcuffing Thomas as he spoke. Apparently, Thomas had been bragging all week to his friends at school that he was going to kill Isaiah while we were away. Isaiah had just had surgery on his shoulder, and his left arm was in a sling. Thomas had decided that he had the physical advantage over him, and with us being away from home, he was provided the perfect opportunity to strike.

It was midafternoon, and Isaiah went into the kitchen with one of his friends along with his girlfriend and his sister, Michal. They had just gotten home from school and were making themselves something to eat. As expected, Thomas had skipped school that day and was sitting in the living room playing video games with his friend when the others had come home. Within minutes, Thomas and Isaiah started arguing.

Thomas went into the kitchen all riled up and started mocking Isaiah for having his arm in a sling. His friend, knowing his intentions, kept telling Thomas not to do it but otherwise didn't intervene. That's when Thomas threatened to stab Isaiah and then lunged to pull the butcher knife out of the kitchen drawer. Isaiah was quick to act and caused Thomas to miss his mark and pull out a set of tongs to stab him with instead. A physical fight ensued, and Isaiah ended up wrestling Thomas to the floor while the police were called.

We pulled off the highway to speak with the arresting officer and with each of our kids. Having to call the police was stressful for them. Of course, they weren't sure how to handle being questioned by the police officers. We called a couple of pastor friends from our church and asked them to go to our home to help them complete their statements and to make sure everyone was okay. We were hours away and just thankful that Isaiah hadn't been seriously injured. We called our case manager to let him know what had happened and that Thomas had been arrested and taken to juvenile detention.

Once Thomas was removed and we were assured that everyone was safe, we continued on our way. Two hours later, the detention center called and asked us to come pick Thomas up. Our oldest son was of legal age and able to do so, but we absolutely refused to let him. Thomas had just fully intended to stab his brother. Why in the world would it be safe to have him come back to the house after only two hours? A planned and executed homicide, even a poorly executed one, still speaks to intent. It was absolutely unacceptable to have him back in our home even if we were there, let alone with us gone.

Christopher continued to argue with the detention staff and refused to have someone come and pick him up. They threatened us with charges of abandonment and insisted Thomas was being released. Since he didn't actually grab the knife, they didn't consider him to be a real threat to the family. As far as they were concerned, he hadn't done anything heinous enough to be retained any longer. They were prepared to transport him home and just drop him off at the door if we continued to refuse to have someone pick him up.

At the very least, we knew Thomas needed to be placed on a psychiatric hold. The last thing we needed was for Thomas to return home and pick up right where he left off. The other children were relieved he was gone, and there was no way I wanted him back home, even if my husband and I were there. We had expected Thomas to be retained at least overnight. We didn't know that they could book and discharge a youth so quickly.

With our continued refusal, they agreed to give us a few hours to explore other options. Thomas's case manager was already working on our behalf to get him transferred to a psychiatric facility for a few days. Within a few hours, we had a transfer in place where Jacob could pick him up from the detention facility and admit him right into the psychiatric facility. Thomas remained there for a week. We made it back home, and he was discharged few days later.

Thomas had an arraignment scheduled the following week for his assault against Isaiah. A public defender was assigned to represent him, and we had little say or involvement with any of their discussions or courts decisions, even though he was a minor and had no idea what was happening around him. He was placed in a youth offender program with the Department of Juvenile Justice, where he was expected to write letters of apology and take a tour of the prison system as a deterrent for future misconduct. None of that happened, of course. The only benefit we saw was that the court process seemed to scare him a little bit.

Just four weeks later, one of our financial partners blessed us with a weekend getaway. Our leaders had been after us for some time to step away and rest. We were both feeling overwhelmed and exhausted with everything that had been happening, especially my husband. He felt like he was drowning. It seemed like all we were doing was working and then dragging Thomas to his weekly doctor appointments, court hearings, and therapy sessions on repeat. A weekend away was exactly what we needed, but we knew it wasn't without risk. Every day had become a risk at this point.

This time, we made sure Michal was out of the house and staying with a friend, and Isaiah was working and had a car to come and go as he needed where he could avoid Thomas. We asked Jacob to come home from college and keep an eye on things, but to not really engage Thomas or pick a fight with him in any way so that there was relative peace while we were away. We didn't venture too far, and thankfully we didn't receive any distressing phone calls. When we returned, we sat down as a family to debrief the weekend, as was our normal practice. Thomas was in his bedroom, refusing to participate, but he had his door open so he could hear what everyone had to say.

I asked Jacob how things had been, and he proceeded to tell us how Thomas had attacked him and thrown a heavy box of Dominoes at his face. I asked him what he did in return, and he said that he had done nothing. I had spent years training the older boys to restrain themselves when it came to Thomas, but now they had all grown to adult size, and Thomas had become very strong. Jacob is a second-degree black belt in tae kwon do, so I knew he could adequately protect himself. He could easily hurt Thomas, but he could also restrain himself when necessary.

I told him to no longer allow Thomas to abuse him in any way. Everyone was too old for that now, and we could no longer be passive about his threats. I told Jacob that the next time Thomas tried to assault him, he was to stop him. All of a sudden, we heard a crash from Thomas's bedroom. When I went down the hallway to see what he had done, one of his dresser drawers had been smashed against the wall, and splintered wood was scattered all over his room. Thomas was furious that I had told Jacob to fight back and protect himself. He started screaming that Jacob was telling lies.

Without saying a word, I turned around and went back into the living room to explain what the crash was about, and Thomas came storming out after me, ready to fight. He was yelling at me with his fists clinched, ready to swing, but Jacob stepped between us and calmly held his hand up in Thomas's direction and said, "You are not going to hit my mother." With that, Thomas swung at Jacob. Jacob blocked and then hit him in return. That's when the real fight began. Isaiah wasn't going to sit there and watch Thomas try to hurt his brother, so he jumped in the fight too. My husband grabbed his phone to call the police.

Christopher could have stepped in to stop it, but he had learned to be especially careful to not lay a finger on Thomas because he could get arrested for abuse and be charged with assault on a minor child. Instead, he chose to step out into the front yard to speak to the 911 dispatcher while I stayed close by to watch over the fight and make sure the boys didn't break anything in the house or each other.

When the police arrived, Thomas was handcuffed and placed in the back of the police car. They questioned each of us and then took Thomas to juvenile detention. Thomas was charged with battery against Jacob, and both police officers reported me for child abuse because I had encouraged Jacob to fight back the next time Thomas tried to attack him. This incident led to an investigation where our children were questioned by Children Services, our home was inspected, and our friends were contacted and questioned about my character and parenting ability. After a few months, the case was closed, but the investigation only served to increase everyone's growing resentment toward Thomas.

This second incident, only weeks after the first one, was exactly what I had been waiting for to be able to justify the need of placing Thomas in a long-term therapeutic group home. I had been asking Christopher to help me get him removed from our home for a while now, but up until then, my husband wasn't ready to send Thomas to live somewhere else. He wanted to keep him at home with us as long as possible. I, on the other hand, wanted him to live somewhere else where he couldn't harm any of us.

Even if Christopher had wanted to send him away beforehand, you don't just send a child to a treatment center. It takes a lot of planning and doctor referrals to even get to the point of getting him on a waiting list. I had already been researching our options for some time so that we were informed and prepared when the time came. All the private group homes I could find ask if your child has ever been violent or started fires. Even if we could afford the $30,000 it would take to admit him, he wouldn't be able to pass the intake questionnaire. Group homes like that are ill equipped to deal with Thomas-type issues.

Many people, including family members, had been suggesting for some time that we send Thomas away to a military school. The idea is that they would be able to shape him up and break his defiant attitude. The military is not where you send the mentally ill. They would never admit him, first of all, and the last thing you would want to do is put a mentally ill person through that kind of emotional and physical conditioning and then give them access to weapons.

Both incidents, and the possibility of what could have happened to Isaiah, were terrifying to think about; but until Thomas started actually escalating beyond threats, we had been stuck without the necessary cause to do anything further to help him or to protect ourselves. He was too violent to go to a private facility, but not violent enough to warrant occupying a bed at a state-recognized facility. We actually needed him to do what he did. Finally, we had two situations that warranted a referral to SIPP or the Statewide In-Patient Psychiatric Program.

Our case manager was able to get Thomas admitted straight from juvenile detention to the psychiatric facility again. From there, we sent him to a youth crisis center which is a short-term, live-in program that offers respite to families in crisis. Teens are usually admitted for only a week or two at a time. We quickly found out that it takes more than a week or two to get everything in place for a long-term facility placement, which was our goal. Just finding an open bed is difficult enough, and the few facilities in our area have perpetual waiting lists. We were racing against the clock. We needed him out of our home, and he needed intensive therapy in a safe and secure environment.

Thomas will never understand the measures we have had to take to keep him safe or to keep ourselves safe. We knew that bringing him home in the interim between the crisis center and the long-term treatment facility would be detrimental because he would come home on his best behavior, especially with it being Christmas and birthday season. It would take some time for him to spiral out of control again, and if we sent him away while he was being "good," he wouldn't be able to understand that getting him admitted had actually been in the works for months and was not related to his behavior on that one particular day.

We fought to keep him in the crisis center for as long as we could. His stay ended up being extended to four weeks, and when they would not allow him to remain any longer, we chose to place him into a foster home. This was a very difficult decision that crushed my husband, but we felt it was the best option we had. We needed to put the needs of our other children first. Their fear and anxiety at the thought of Thomas coming back home was too great to dismiss. We knew a bed was opening in a couple of weeks and that his placement in foster care would only be temporary. In the meantime, we continued to work with the SIPP team in getting all the necessary paperwork and funding in place for his upcoming admittance.

CHAPTER 15

Those who hope in the Lord will renew
their strength. They will soar on wings like eagles.
—Isaiah 40:31

Thomas was very upset when we had to explain to him that he was not coming home with us but was instead going to live with a foster family. He felt he had been working hard to prove to us that he was ready to come home again even though we had witnessed no such effort. After five weeks in three different facilities, he had not acknowledged the incidents that had gotten him arrested. He had made no attempt to apologize or even discuss the matter. Instead, he had been refusing to speak with us unless he was forced or he wanted something from us. Simply living apart and not causing any problems seemed to be proof enough in his mind that he had changed and was ready to be reunited with the family.

When we told him he wasn't coming home, he kept asking us why. He honestly didn't understand what made this time any different than all the previous times we had him institutionalized. He had done his time without incident, and history always dictated that he returned home afterward. We kept explaining to him that he had become too violent toward the family and that he was no longer behaving in a safe manner. He couldn't understand. Our conversation went back and forth with him asking us why again and again and us trying our best to explain our reasons. Our explanations only seemed to bring up his feelings of rejection and abandonment.

Trying to make him understand or see things from our perspective was impossible. His pained expression and the tone of his voice conveyed the hurt he was feeling, which pierced our hearts. The staff could see the tears welling up in our eyes, and they encouraged us that Thomas would be okay, and although we were making a difficult decision, we were doing what needed to be done and what would ultimately be best for him. We knew we were making the right decision. That didn't make it any less difficult.

I was so worn out from our strained relationship and having to continuously advocate and fight for every single service he was receiving. The amount of energy that had to be put into the meetings and phone calls with teachers and treatment staff, the therapy appointments, the pharmacy runs, and his constant troublemaking was absolutely draining. Christopher and I were often at odds with who would answer the phone, sign the updated treatment plans, and who would be tasked with taking him to and from therapy each week. Neither one of us wanted to do any of it anymore.

It crushed Christopher to drop Thomas off at the foster home. It was the last thing he wanted to do, and seeing how dejected Thomas was made it that much harder on him. He still saw Thomas a few times a week whenever he needed to be picked up for an appointment. It was weird having him stay with another family yet still seeing him with regularity. The foster mother would call often, asking for our permission to allow Thomas to go places like basketball games or to the movies with the other teens living in the home with him.

We focused our attention toward getting everything finalized as quickly as possible for his next stage of treatment, but my husband was struggling with feelings of guilt for seemingly abandoning him to the system. I tried to encourage him that he hadn't abandoned Thomas in any way. He was still fighting for him every single day and trying to do what was best for him. Of course, Christopher knew all of that, but there are still difficult emotions that have to be processed through when you're dealing with a family member that requires you to make hard decisions on their behalf. Nothing with Thomas came easily or without cost.

Thomas was still attending his regular high school, which was only a few miles from where we lived. To avoid the traffic, the foster mother dropped him off at a gas station down the street from the school and then expected him to choose to walk to class from there.

On mornings where we hadn't left for the office yet, we would catch him walking up to the neighbor's house across the street. We knew he would end up spending the day there sleeping, playing video games, smoking weed, and running around. The other boy's father worked a lot and didn't seem to be around much to ensure his son went to school, so he and Thomas were a perfect match for each other.

The few times Thomas actually remained on campus, our daughter witnessed him trying to sell weed to some of the other students in her gym class. A few of her friends snapped pictures of him walking the hallways because of the crazy way he looked. He was made fun of a lot for his appearance, but I believe he was oblivious. He was definitely a sight to behold with his baggy pants pulled down below his butt and his oversized T-shirts that just about hung to his knees. He often wore white socks with black sandals on his feet to avoid the peer pressure of not having the newest and most expensive pair of gym shoes.

He always looked disheveled with his wrinkly clothes and his dirty hair tied up in multiple rubber-band tuffs all over his head. He seemed determined to achieve a Coolio hairstyle. It took him over a year to realize that his thick, silky Native American hair couldn't dread and stick up that way. His skin stayed red and blotchy all year long with eczema rashes that he refused to medicate. They would be most prevalent at the bend of his elbows, between his fingers, and around his mouth. His appearance embarrassed his siblings greatly.

After his few short stays in juvenile detention, Thomas had begun to identify with having a "thug life." He started speaking with a lot of urban slag, started strutting when he walked, and he altered the way he was dressing, which drove the family crazy. He had acquired a thick chain necklace and carried a large pocketknife wherever he went. When he was very little, he lived on a small rural horse ranch. With us, he grew up in suburban America and for many years lived on the edge of a golf course. He has never known a thug day in his life.

Around the same time, he started introducing himself to everyone as Toby. We heard from the neighbor that when the other teens in the detention center asked him his name and he told them it was Thomas, one of them said that he didn't look like a Thomas. Apparently, the other boy thought he looks more like a Toby. I don't know what the difference is from Thomas to Toby. Maybe Toby sounded a little tougher. Whatever the reason, from that moment on, Thomas started identifying as a Toby.

After only three weeks, everything was in place and ready for him to be admitted. We made arrangements to pick him up from the foster family's home that weekend. In addition to his duffel bag, he came out of the house with a trash bag overflowing with clothes. Apparently, his wardrobe had drastically expanded. He hugged the other teens and said goodbye to them like they had become the best of friends. He smiled proudly when he introduced us to another boy as being his brother. I could see the instant and deep connection he felt toward him, but seeing the way he was acting made me angry. He had two brothers already.

I wasn't upset that he had found a comrade or that they had connected and shared something together. It was just upsetting to repeatedly see the way he would interact with other people contrary to the way he interacted with the family. Those other people are the only ones who seem to "get him" and who he feels are good to him. Whenever he speaks of other people like that, he gets this giddy way about him that makes me so angry. It's hard to explain. I guess unless you experience it, you probably can't understand, and it's hard to put it into words without sounding like a jealous lunatic.

Thomas has always looked at us as if we were his captors and that his brothers only exist to torture and abuse him. His brothers have actually been quite good to him, considering all the things he has done to them over the years. Anytime I have seen them really argue or fight with him has been in direct response to something Thomas had started. We spent years trying to explain to him that having older brothers who want to wrestle and pick on him from time to time was completely normal. They weren't being mean; they were being big brothers.

As we drove away from the house that day, Christopher started asking Thomas questions about the foster family and if he had a good time with them. His father has been the only one who could successfully break the silence and pull some sort of conversation out of him. Getting Thomas to speak to us at all only happened with great persistence. Getting him to open up and share his feelings about anything was a triumph.

Whenever I have been alone with him in the car, he has insisted on sitting in the back seat where he would fall asleep or pretend I wasn't trying to engage him in conversation. Going to and from appointments provided us the perfect opportunity to spend some quality time together. Our other children took full advantage of any and all alone time, but Thomas didn't speak unless you asked him a direct question—sometimes repeatedly. I might get a yes or no answer, but it was usually a simple shoulder shrug.

This time was different. Thomas was very open about how amazing the foster family had been. I could see the hurt in my husband's eyes as he explained how the foster dad was so cool and awesome and how well he had treated him. The other teens staying there had become his real family—as if we were his fake family. We could see how much he had enjoyed it in the end.

If I was him, I probably would have loved it too. He got to skip school without anyone following up with him or questioning where he had been all day. He got to attend some sporting events, go to the movies, got a bunch of new clothes. He even got to eat out a few times. Life was good. He had adults there to make sure his daily needs were met, but no real demands had been placed on him.

I was too hurt to contribute positively to the conversation. Everything that came to my mind kept starting with, *Really!* I figured it was best that I kept my mouth shut. We needed to keep the car ride as pleasant as possible. Now was not the time to object or tick him off. Pretty much anything I said that was contrary to his own way of thinking resulted in war. We needed to be able to get him to the facility and admit him without issue.

He has never been aware of the pain he has caused us. I have had to continually remind myself of that. We had been the ones who fought to bring him home. We were the ones who struggled to bring some stability to his life. We were the ones who provided him with a family and who spoke love and peace over him. We were the ones. In return, we were the ones whom he rejected. We were the ones who paid the price. We were the ones who repeatedly laid our lives down in sacrifice to his own.

*****

After we dropped Thomas off at the treatment center and we signed all of the paperwork, completed the facility tour, and went over all the rules, I left to attend a women's conference with a few of my colleagues. Everything had been nonstop all day long, and there hadn't been a moment to decompress or even process the fact that we had finally accomplished what we had been fighting so hard to achieve for months. I felt like I had been in a long battle, both spiritually and physically, and a cease fire had finally been issued.

When the worship music started to play, my eyes welled up with tears. I had felt weepy for hours, and being able to stop for a moment and process how I was feeling opened up the floodgates of every emotion I had been holding inside for so long. Tears started rolling down my cheeks, and no matter how hard I tried, I couldn't do anything to stop them. The dam had finally been broken, and for the first time in months, I felt like I could finally breathe.

As I pressed into the presence of the Lord, I could feel His comfort in a way that I hadn't allowed myself to feel in a long time. All the pain and anxiety, the stress and the constant worry, the sorrow and grief had all been suffocating me; but in order for me to keep going, to keep fighting, to keep pressing onward, I had to remain strong and keep standing. Now I felt like I could finally take a moment to rest. The objective had been achieved. Mine and my family's safety was no longer at stake. Thomas was safe. We were safe. Pause. Breathe.

CHAPTER 16

I will restore you to health and heal your wounds,
declares the Lord.
—Jeremiah 30:17

Occasionally, people have stopped to ask me how I was feeling with everything we were going through. That has been one of the hardest questions for me to answer. One minute I'm so angry I could hit him; and the next, I'm so heartbroken over his brokenness. I could hate him one minute and then pity him for how bound up and deceived he is in the next. I just started answering that I felt *yes*. When they would look at me strangely, I would tell them that whatever emotion they guessed that I was feeling, the simplest answer I could give them would be yes. I feel all of them—sometimes all at the same time.

Trauma is processed so differently person to person. I think Christopher and I have rarely been in the same place at the same time emotionally. We've each had to process through our own identities as a mother and a father, which has been a challenge at times because he grew up without a father, and I grew up without a mother. We didn't have that parent around to model ourselves after. We didn't have that parent to go to for wisdom or encouragement. We didn't know anyone else who had experienced what we were going through or even walked a similar path to ours.

I think we can both say that we've been excellent parents, but it hasn't been without a good deal of self-evaluation. I think any time you have a child screaming at you that they hate you and that you're the worst person in the world will cause you to pause and evaluate yourself. At least it did with us. For a while, we were constantly asking ourselves if we were being the best kind of parents for Thomas.

Were we being the best kind of parents to the other three, and what could we be doing differently?

This process has helped us both to not be so judgmental toward other parents. You just don't know what goes on in other families behind closed doors. You don't know what the other person is walking through. Our experience has given me a greater sense of grace toward others and has allowed me to consider other factors at work than what I might be witnessing in the middle of a grocery-store meltdown. It has even given me a greater grace with the "healthy" or "normal" kids within a family dynamic like ours. I have seen the struggle our other three children have had growing up with a mentally ill and destructive sibling.

It wasn't until Thomas was admitted and safely locked away from the family long-term that I was able to really step back and see the extent of the trauma he had inflicted. Just our daily stress level alone had wrecked us physically. We had stopped taking care of ourselves at some point along the way. Our sleep patterns were all skewed, and we had been stress eating and gaining weight for months. Once our daughter knew she was safe and that he would be gone long-term, she immediately crashed. Her immune system completely shut down, and she was in full-blown adrenal fatigue.

She couldn't stop crying, and she became so sick that she wasn't able to get out of bed for weeks. She was no longer emotionally or physically able to keep up with the demands of her rigorous academic schedule. She had no choice but to drop out of her accelerated program. I ended up withdrawing her from high school and allowing her a few months to rest while I switched her to a free-form, part-time program she could complete online. She had very few requirements left to graduate as a result of the accelerated program she had been in even though she still had two more years of high school ahead of her. She had plenty of time to complete her last few classes, and getting her health stabilized became the priority.

Some researchers say that upward of 75–95 percent of the illnesses that plague our lives are a direct result of our very own thought life. According to Dr. Caroline Leaf, a cognitive neuroscientist, the average person has over thirty thousand thoughts a day; and if those thoughts are toxic, we can create the right type of conditions to become ill with diseases from as serious as cancer, to painful ulcers, to a variety of skin conditions and autoimmune disorders. Thoughts of fear are believed to trigger more than 1,400 known physical and chemical responses in our bodies and activate more than thirty different hormones.

Not only have I been able to see the ill-effects of fear and trauma at work in Thomas's life, but I have also been able to recognize how they have negatively affected the rest of our children. Males and females deal with trauma and toxic thoughts very differently from each other. Females use more of the left side of their brains, which has strong connections to the outer cortex and frontal lobe where they focus more on detail, intuition, and where reasoning is located. Their memories are more connected with emotional events. Males, on the other hand, use more of the right side of their brains when building memory, which makes their memories more practical and event-oriented, requiring less emotion and less words when processing.

Our sons have coped with the ongoing trauma Thomas brought into our home very differently than our daughter. The fact that she is the closest to Thomas in age and that she has spent more time home alone with him than her brothers has greatly affected how she has been able to process the trauma. Not surprisingly, our sons have been able to process through their different experiences with Thomas using a more practical approach than their sister. They have been able to release a lot of their frustration through the many physical altercations that they have had with him over the years.

For instance, after Thomas tried to stab Isaiah, Isaiah had to immediately defend himself to gain physical control over Thomas, or else his life was at risk. Being able to hit Thomas and physically respond to protect himself gave him an immediate outlet to release and overcome his fear. When Thomas came out of his bedroom with the intension of fighting me and Jacob and Isaiah both came to my defense, it ended up being very therapeutic for them to be able to respond physically to protect me as well as the rest of the family. They felt great satisfaction at having been able to overcome the abuser and stop him.

Michal has rarely been able to physically defend herself the way her brothers have. She has always relied on them to be her protectors whenever her father or I have been out of the room or away from the house. She can recall the very first memory where she began to fear Thomas, and it was within the first month of him coming to live with us. She remembers playing with him upstairs in his room, and without warning or provocation, he bit her so hard that he broke the skin, and she began to bleed. I remember when that happened. They were only four and five years old.

When she has described the evil way his face changed in that moment, I have wondered if she was also seeing into the spirit and that the combination of the physical pain and the fear of the demonic have both stayed with her all these years later. Every additional attack he inflicted on her or on someone else in the house only increased her fear and insecurity from that moment forward. As they grew and got older, her brothers were not always around; and by the time they were thirteen and fourteen, Thomas was much taller and stronger than she was.

Whenever she did stand up for herself and challenge Thomas, he would punch her and leave her bruised. He tried to do the same thing to his brothers, but they were quick to hit him back; and with them being a little bit older and stronger than him, they had the upper hand. Subsequently, Michal would avoid Thomas whenever she could and learned to deny herself the things she wanted to do because she didn't want to get hurt for something as simple as wanting a turn to watch a program on television. Over the years, she retreated more and more into her bedroom.

Michal has always enjoyed her bed and her books, so recognizing her retreating as a coping mechanism didn't come to light until the trauma increased and all of us started retreating more and more into our own personal space. Unfortunately, she couldn't avoid him entirely. With only being a year apart, they got up at the same time every morning during their middle school years and attended the same school. Whenever she passed him in the school hallways, she felt anxious, and sometimes he would menace her. With her brothers in high school, they were usually out and about more often than she was, and she would find herself alone in the house with him in the afternoons after school.

Being alone with him didn't mean there was necessarily any direct conflict going on between them, but it did contribute to her overall sense of fear and feelings of being unprotected. She knew that with how unpredictable his behavior was, there was always an element of risk for her. She never knew when an argument would break out and he would hit her or cuss at her. Whenever she would open up to share the anxiety she was experiencing with other peers or adults outside of the immediate family, her feelings were often dismissed or diminished as being dramatic exaggerations.

For years, she kept silent about the bruises on her body, and she stopped expressing any of her own needs. Whenever I would ask her how she was doing, she would tell me that she was fine when, in reality, she was struggling. She had decided that her needs were not as important as Thomas's needs. She knew how much his needs demanded our attention. She could see how emotionally taxing his care was on her father and me. She also saw how financially difficult things had become with relocating and transitioning into a place of faith-based support where providing for everyone's physical needs had also become a strain. She didn't want to further burden us. She started stuffing and ignoring her own needs in sacrifice to everyone else's.

Stuffing her feelings and her fears led to regular panic attacks. She could no longer cope with everyday events, and if her older brothers started wrestling or horsing around in the house, she became very fearful even though she knew it was all in fun. The very sound of horseplay triggered all the times we have had to wrestle with Thomas, as well as the times he had physically assaulted one of us. She would have to go lock herself in her bedroom and stay there until she could convince herself that it was safe enough to come out again.

Michal was displaying symptoms of post-traumatic stress disorder, or more accurately, complex PTSD. Just because someone experiences feelings of fear and has panic attacks doesn't mean they necessarily have PTSD because it is normal to have symptoms of stress and anxiety after any kind of traumatic event. To be diagnosed with

PTSD, you have to meet the specific requirements outlined in the *Diagnostic and Statistical Manual of Mental Disorders*. I have never pursued any kind of official diagnosis for her, nor do I feel it is necessary to do so. At first, it didn't occur to me that our situation could result in symptoms of PTSD for any of us.

Together, she and I have done some research and have been able to identify that she does meet the basic criteria for treatment. A PTSD diagnosis requires that you have to have been directly or indirectly exposed to a traumatic event where the event is experienced again and again through traumatic nightmares, intrusive memories, flashbacks, prolonged distress, or physiologic reactions to trauma related stimuli. These symptoms can then cause avoidance patterns to form where the person persistently makes an effort to avoid any kind of trauma-related thoughts and feelings and particular reminders of things related to the traumatic event itself.

Individuals with PTSD have some sort of negative changes in their mood that worsen after the event and are then displayed through disassociation, negative beliefs about themselves or the world, and persistent emotions such as fear, horror, anger, guilt, or shame. People with PTSD can show disinterest in the things they loved to do before, and they have feelings of being detached and separated from others around them. They can also have ongoing difficulty experiencing any kind of positive emotions, which can lead to severe depression.

To be clinically diagnosed with PTSD, you have to display two or more of the following behaviors, which are aggression or irritability, being self-destructive or reckless, being hypervigilant, having an exaggerated startle response, ongoing problems concentrating, and sleep disturbance. These negative symptoms must last for more than a month, and they must also show impairment that these factors are interfering with your social life or your occupation. These struggles must not be due to any kind of medication, substance use, or be caused by any kind of illness. Unfortunately, Michal meets all of these determining factors.

Many doctors are starting to distinguish between PTSD and complex PTSD when treating patients, although complex PTSD is not listed as an official disorder. While post-traumatic stress disorder occurs from a single, onetime traumatic event such as an earthquake, a terrorist attack, a car accident, or rape, complex PTSD occurs from chronic, ongoing trauma that can reoccur for months or even years.

The ongoing trauma might be due to factors such as domestic violence, long-term sexual abuse, being held in a concentration camp, being a prisoner of war, prostitution, and human trafficking—any situation where the victim is held physically or emotionally captive and under the perpetrator's control where they are unable to get away. People who experience chronic trauma, especially as children, often report additional symptoms not listed in a standard PTSD diagnosis that require additional considerations during treatment. This is what has led to some doctors identifying a complex PTSD.

Once Michal emotionally and physically crashed, I devoted my time to getting her health back on track. It was during these many doctor visits that I learned just how much she was dealing with anxiety and how little she was actually sleeping. It took over a year for her hormone levels to balance out and for her sleeping to become a little more regulated, although she still struggles with sleeping to this day. She didn't want to take any kind of mood stabilizers to help her cope, so we focused on a more holistic approach with vitamins and herbs and getting her to talk through some of the things she had stuffed and ignored for years.

Michal was serving with a local ministry, and it wasn't until one of her interns called me and asked me to come see her that I learned that Michal had been dealing with thoughts of suicide. She had already gone through a period of time where she felt so depressed that she was cutting herself, but I never would have guessed in a million years that she was also dealing with suicidal thoughts. I was so relieved she had confided in someone she trusted, but at the same time, I felt betrayed that she had kept it a secret from me when we regularly stayed up late into the night talking and processing through everything. I guess everything but that.

Michal told me that she had made a plan to kill herself one day while everyone was out of the house, but she ended up attending a youth event the night before where the speaker addressed suicide and then invited anyone dealing with suicidal thoughts to come forward and receive prayer. She went forward that night. She says it was the first time she had been honest about it and brave enough to acknowledge it publicly. None of the youth leaders notified me or her father. She later said that the youth pastor never followed up with her about how she was doing after that evening.

I had already forced her to see a counselor a few times, but I knew it was time to find her some ongoing professional help. I was suddenly afraid to leave her alone. I finally had Thomas in a contained and safe environment where he couldn't hurt himself or the family. I couldn't bear the thought of her harming herself now that she was finally safe. I knew I couldn't watch her twenty-four hours a day. I prayed for the Lord to send an angel to be with her whenever she felt alone and depressed. I had to believe that with her finally opening up, she would only get better and the worst was now behind her.

CHAPTER 17

Listen, my son, to your father's instruction
and do not forsake your mother's teaching.
—Proverbs 1:8–9

We met with the treatment team at the new facility to have an introductory meeting to discuss Thomas and his treatment plan over the next twelve to eighteen months. We were instructed to go over Thomas's positive and negative traits and areas we wanted him to improve in. Christopher proceeded to outline his cyclical behaviors and let them know to expect him to behave very well initially. He told the behavioral therapist that Thomas will be on his best behavior for about the first three months. Long enough for him to learn the lay of the land and begin to feel comfortable.

The behavioral therapist was very blunt and direct. He didn't hesitate to express his disbelief in what he was being told. We knew there was nothing more we could say that would convince him otherwise. As always, time would tell. This wasn't the first time someone didn't believe us. We had learned to expect it. Thomas was then invited into the room to join the discussion, but he refused to answer any questions or contribute his thoughts to the conversation in any way. This frustrated the behavioral therapist all the more.

After a few weeks, we began family therapy sessions with their in-house therapist. She began our sessions with asking us to share our adoption story with her and Thomas. After we explained that Thomas was biologically my nephew and that his birth father was my brother, the therapist stopped me and asked me to repeat that again. Thomas had been telling her that he was different than the rest of us. That he didn't belong and that we didn't understand him. He said we

167

hadn't allowed him to be his own individual within the family and that he felt like an outsider.

When she pointed out to him that he wasn't in reality different from the rest of us because we were all related even before the adoption took place, Thomas seemed surprised by that revelation. I'm not sure why because we have never kept his origins a secret, and he has a very detailed scrapbook that tells his birth story. His scrapbook is full of baby pictures, pictures of the houseboating trip, and pictures of the time we went to visit him while he was in the foster home. He used to look at it all the time. We also had many conversations over the years about his biological parents.

We then went through all the ways that each of us are similar and different from each other. Dad and Isaiah are very early risers. Michal is a night owl. Jacob is an introvert while Isaiah has never known a stranger. Thomas loves music and draws well just like me. On and on, we went in effort to show him that we have our individual differences from one another, but we also have many likes and dislikes in common. Shifting his mind-set and changing his distorted identity was the initial focus of our family sessions, which had never been discussed in family therapy before. I was encouraged and hoped that it would make a lasting impact with his thinking.

As expected, Thomas was a model prisoner from February through the beginning of May. His treatment team said they didn't understand why Thomas was even there because they weren't seeing any of the behaviors that caused the SIPP team to initiate his placement. Thomas was fulfilling all of his daily requirements and had been moving up in rank in response to his positive behaviors. He achieved the highest rank, which allowed him to have the most freedom and the best privileges. Once he remained there for a couple of weeks, he became angry that he wasn't released to return home. He told his therapist that working the program didn't get him what he wanted, so he left her office and immediately punched another boy in the face.

He was only holding himself together because he thought it would allow him to return home. From that day forward, he checked out of participating in any of the group therapy sessions other than to jump in and argue with something another boy had shared. He refused to complete any of his schoolwork and became very aggressive toward the teacher, which included cussing at her and walking out of the classroom. He told the staff that he didn't want us to come and visit him, and he started refusing to attend our weekly therapy sessions. Instead, he sat in his room until we left.

As part of the process of reintegration back into family life, everyone in the program is required to call home every week. After months, Thomas was still refusing to comply. On weeks where he had gained enough good behavior points to leave campus on a family outing for a few hours, he refused to let us pick him up even after offering to take him to his favorite restaurant for lunch. It was clear he had no interest in being around any of us or repairing our relationship in any way.

Fighting became an ongoing problem for Thomas, and his personal therapy sessions became more about his daily conflicts with the other boys than on anything involving his past. He ended up getting arrested for assaulting one of the male workers, which involved Thomas hitting him with a chair. An investigation of the incident was launched, and Thomas was found to be at fault, but the worker had to be reassigned to another facility due to their safety policy. Unfortunately, his outburst caused occupational consequences for that staff member, who was not at fault in any way.

Shortly after that, Thomas got upset and broke a plastic mirror and slashed himself across the chest. He later said he didn't know why he did it. The behavioral therapist apologized to my husband for not believing him and said that everything he had told him to expect to happen was now happening. He went on to say that Thomas was not working the program, and he wasn't sure how much longer they could continue to keep him when there was a long waiting list of others who needed their help. Basically, they couldn't help him if he wasn't willing to be helped. My hope of this program making a difference for Thomas long-term started slipping away.

During this time, we were in full-blown wedding planning mode for our son, Isaiah. He was getting married the first week of August, and we weren't sure what to do with regard to Thomas. He was still refusing to speak with us, but he had attended a few of our family sessions in silence with no forward progress being made. We honestly didn't know if he even cared that his brother was getting married. This was a major family event, and normally, this wasn't something a brother would miss, but Thomas wasn't an ordinary brother. His therapist was excited about the wedding and brought it up often to try to get Thomas excited too. She was the driving force behind encouraging him to attend.

The thought of having Thomas there brought up many concerns. I knew there was no way I could keep an eye on him in the midst of all the festivities. I didn't expect Thomas to necessarily do anything wrong, but you just never knew with him. His very presence caused the family anxiety. He could pick a fight, he could run away, or he could be perfectly fine. If he didn't want to go, that alone could cause issue. After voicing our concerns with his therapist, she offered to chaperon him to and from the wedding. Knowing that he was there with someone he liked that could also keep an eye on him made all the difference.

On the day of the wedding, Thomas came and seemed to be genuinely happy for his brother. Isaiah was pleased that he was able to make it. They had a brief moment together after the ceremony where Thomas congratulated him and they got their picture taken together. Thomas didn't speak to the rest of us at all that day other than to respond to his father's initial greeting when he had arrived. He didn't approach his other brother or sister and he kept his distance during the reception. He spent most of the reception observing from the balcony with some of his younger cousins.

Since Thomas did well that day, the therapist was convinced that he would do fine being released and sent back home. His twelve-to eighteen-month treatment program was instantly reduced to only six months. I couldn't understand how she viewed him safe when he wasn't making any real personal progress. He had continued to have conflict with the other people in the program. He hadn't interacted with any of his immediate family at the wedding other than to briefly congratulate his brother and his new bride. It seemed to me that she was making her determination from a single family event that was surrounded with a lot of joy and celebration, which is completely separate from daily life.

His grandparents and his aunts and uncles and cousins had all greeted him and hugged on him during the wedding reception. Maybe she was basing some of her assessment off that, but other family members loving on him was no reflection on his own behavior. His time with the extended family has been short over the years. Family gatherings have usually revolved around holidays and birthday celebrations. He has never had much opportunity to have issues with any of them, and RAD children don't usually have conflict with others not intimately involved in their lives on a continual basis. We were living hundreds of miles away from all of them.

Regardless, we knew his time in the facility had been growing short because of his lack of participation. The wedding just seemed to be the final catalyst that got him discharged. His sister was panicked at the news of him coming home, but there was nothing we could do to stop it. Our case manager immediately started working to find another treatment facility, but we knew it would take time. If another placement was found, he would be added to a waiting list. There would be no telling how long it would take for a bed to open up. The very thought of us going back into the Thomas cycle was overwhelming.

He came home right at the beginning of a new school year. He was repeating the ninth grade for the second time. His father enrolled him back at his regular high school. Right after enrollment, Thomas was sent from the administration office to class, but he never showed up. He actually never attended a single class that fall even though we created a safety plan with his IEP team, and Thomas had signed it and knew exactly what was expected of him. Sadly, his teachers that didn't already know him from the previous school year had no idea who he was and what he even looked like.

We continued to force him to get up each morning for school. We drove him there ourselves and dropped him off at the front door where he was met by an administrator who was assigned to then walk him directly to his first period class. At first, he refused to get out of the car. He was furious that someone was there waiting on him because he had no intention of going to class. I think he followed the administrator inside for a day or two before he started refusing to go into the building at all.

It got to the point that he would get out of the car and just stand unmoving on the sidewalk. The administrator would stand there encouraging him to walk with him, but Thomas would remain frozen in place, evaluating his options. Students would be shuffling past us, but he would stand there well past the sound of the late bell. I could tell Thomas felt trapped, and by us trying to make him go to school, I knew we were pushing him to a dangerous place—but what alternative did we have? He was fifteen years old, and he needed to go to school. We were setting him up to make good choices, but he simply wouldn't do it.

The high school was very large with many buildings on the campus. Thomas continued to refuse to follow the administrator into the main lobby. Instead, he started walking away and merging into the heavy flow of students that were going around the main building toward the back of the campus. Within minutes, he would disappear into the crowd. We knew he wasn't going to class. He was going to keep on walking past the buildings and onward through the neighborhood.

Every morning we repeated the same ridiculous pattern. I kept waiting for him to refuse to get out of bed, but he never did. He would get into the car every day. We would pull up to the curb. He would get out of the car, stand there for a second, look around, and then off he went. When he was confident that we weren't going to try to stop him, he stopped pretending by going around the building. Instead, he walked right across the parking lot, past the police officers, and right down the main street. We did this week after week, every single morning. The only difference this time was that we had a school paying attention and documenting that his lack of attendance wasn't due to any negligence on our part.

He would spend his days with the neighbor at his house, or he would just wander around the neighborhood. Sometimes he would hang out at the local parks with the other kids who were cutting class. We would hear of his antics every now and then. He was stealing things, hanging out with the drug dealers, and getting high almost every day. He would come home in the evenings without a word, and we would begin the same process all over again in the morning.

We did our best to not confront him or stir up any conflict of any kind. We were not willing to get back into the violence cycle with him again. The atmosphere in the house had shifted back to the heaviness we knew all too well. His demons had grown stronger, and whenever he was home, I could see how uneasy he was with being there.

In addition to all the negative feelings he had toward us in the natural, I could see how spiritually unsettled he was to be in our presence. He kind of twitched and fidgeted. He did everything he could to not engage us in any way. He kept his eyes down and his mouth shut. He seemed absolutely miserable. We were counting the days until we could get him into another facility.

CHAPTER 18

"For I know the plans I have for you," declares the Lord,
"plans to prosper you and not to harm you,
plans to give you hope and a future.
—Jeremiah 29:11

Thomas was home with us for three months when we received the phone call notifying us that a bed had finally opened up and that we could admit him into the next long-term treatment facility that weekend. I was hopeful that this next placement would get us a little closer to his eighteenth birthday, where he would be free to go live his life as he saw fit, and we would no longer be legally responsible for any of his actions.

There was no way Thomas was going to go willingly. We had to devise a way to get him into the car and get him all the way there without him knowing our plans ahead of time. I didn't want to deceive him, but he would never get in the car if he knew our intentions. Since he was overdue for a haircut, I thought taking him to get one would be the perfect reason for him to go somewhere with us. We waited until that morning to wake him up and ask him if he wanted to go. He agreed, and I was extremely anxious the whole morning, waiting to see if he would actually get up and get in the car with us. To my surprise, he did.

After the haircut, we headed straight to the facility. I know Thomas was expecting to head back to the house; and after a while, I could tell that he wanted to ask us where we were going, but he didn't say a word. We were over halfway there before his father decided it was time to tell him where we were going. We chose to drive Christopher's sports car that only had two doors so that it would make it impossible for Thomas to jump and run from the car. We had to prepare for every scenario because we expected him to flip out when we told him.

Sure enough, he became very upset, which I completely understood. He started screaming and cussing at us, and he did try to find a way to open the driver's-side door to flee. For a moment, I was afraid he was going to start hitting us. We had made it where he couldn't get out of the car, but that also meant we were confined within his reaction space. For a second, I visualized him causing us to lose control of the vehicle and crashing on the highway. I immediately started praying for peace and protection. Once he realized he had nowhere to go, he sat back and started crying. We did our best to explain to him why we were placing him in yet another group home. We painted everything in the most positive light that we could.

As soon as we pulled into the parking lot and opened the car door, Thomas got out, surveyed his surroundings, and then sprinted away. Some of the staff went out looking for him, but they couldn't find him. We went inside, and the program director called the police. It didn't take very long for the officers to come walking through the door with Thomas in handcuffs. He had done his best to resist them, and he was out of breath and a little disheveled. The officers made it very clear that they would not hesitate to lock him up for a while if he tried to run away again.

Before they left, the officers spent some time trying to reason with Thomas. They told him he was only there because his parents obviously loved and cared for him very much. They told him that we were only trying to do what was best for him. Thomas was quick to shake his head and retort that we have never loved him. It stung to hear him say what we already knew he believed, but already knowing it didn't make his words hurt any less. Thomas was furious with everyone, but the threat of being taken to detention kept him from running away when they finally removed the handcuffs.

We went through a large stack of intake paperwork while Thomas was escorted to the house where he would be staying. This facility was not a locked-down facility like his previous placement. Here he would have the freedom to move around. They had a good-sized campus that had very nice amenities, which included a swimming pool and a full-size basketball court. It made me nervous that he would have the ability to just walk out the front door anytime he wanted, but I was pleased that he would be staying in such a nice place.

The instant we were introduced to his therapist, my husband and I didn't like her. We knew Thomas wasn't going to like her either. There was just something about her. His houseparents, on the other hand, were very kind and welcoming, and they immediately put me at ease. We knew he was going to really like them as soon as they introduced themselves. The house Thomas was going to be staying in had a large living room with a fireplace and vaulted ceilings just like a family home. It was much more inviting than the previous facility, which was much older and set up more like an institution.

Thomas refused to look at us when we left, but we weren't expecting him to, considering the circumstances. We didn't go and see him for the first two weeks as instructed so that he could acclimate to his new living situation. Thomas was enrolled for school at a local high school not too far away, and he rode a bus back and forth with the other boys. I wondered how long it was going to take him to start skipping. I figured as long as it took for him to devise a strategy of how to get out and where to go.

When it came time to begin our weekly therapy sessions, we were told that Thomas was refusing to meet with us or speak to us on the phone. We weren't particularly surprised because he had refused to see us many times in the previous placement. He had also spent the last few months at home doing his best to ignore us. I assumed he was still angry. Christopher checked in with his therapist a few times a week, hoping to be told that Thomas was ready. We didn't want to make the nearly two-hour drive one-way to be turned away upon our arrival. One week turned into six. When Christmas finally rolled around, we decided to buy him a present and go and see him even if he didn't want us to.

It was extremely awkward between us when we arrived. Thomas showed us around the house and introduced us to some of the other boys. He had been cleaning the bathrooms and helping with some basic chores to earn some money. He was proud to tell us that he was working a little bit and had his own bank account. This group home focused on teaching their youth how to transition into adulthood, so Thomas was being introduced to opportunities he had never had before, and he seemed to really want to please his houseparents, whom he liked very much.

I was eager to see Thomas's reaction to his Christmas gift. I bought him a very expensive pair of Jordan high-tops, which is something I knew he would really like and the one thing we always fought over when he was younger. I had expected him to smile or something when he opened it, but instead I barely got a reaction. He mumbled a thank-you and set them aside. I hoped he liked them, but I never saw him wear them. I figured it was a typical RAD response, or maybe our past battles over shoes had ruined it. I don't know, but I never saw those shoes again.

After an awkward pause, he went on to tell us about all the gifts he had received over the past few weeks from some of the program's sponsors. He had a bunch of new clothes hanging in his closet and a nice new blanket on his bed. He showed us his new football, his ten-inch tablet, and the brand-new laptop computer he had been given. Then he walked us outside so that we could see his new bicycle and the skateboard that he had been learning to ride. I wasn't convinced that giving Thomas a means of escape and access to electronic communication was wise, but the gifts were very nice.

We had a stolen phone at the house that Thomas had left behind. It was logged into his secret Facebook and Messenger accounts. Every now and then Christopher, would charge it up to see what Thomas was up to since he now had access to be online with his new electronics. Most of Thomas's conversations revolved around the desire to return home so that he could smoke weed. He kept asking his friend when he was going to come and pick him up. His friend didn't have a car—I'm not so sure he even had his license—so there was a lot of discussion on who he could get to drive him the two hours to pick him up.

We called to let his therapist know that he was actively planning an escape. It wasn't long after that when we received a call that

Thomas and another boy had run away together. They had skipped all of their classes at school that day, and neither one of them came back on the bus that afternoon. The staff called the police, but there was nothing else to do but wait to see if they turned back up again. Thomas had somehow gotten his hands on a cell phone. We were able to monitor the conversation he was having with the neighbor boy for a few hours before he either lost access to WIFI or the cell phone died.

The other boy who had run away with him returned to the group home late that same evening. He told the houseparents how they had left the school together and then spent the day hiding out in the woods, waiting for a ride to show up. The other boy had gotten hungry and scared, so he decided to turn back. From the messages we had been following that day, Thomas's escape plan wasn't working out the way he had hoped. His friend had messaged to say that he had asked his sister's boyfriend to drive him down to pick him up, but there was delay after delay. His perfect plan had started to unravel.

Thomas returned to the group home the following day dirty and hungry. His ride had never shown up. He refused to answer any of the houseparents' questions. I imagine he was embarrassed and very upset with the way everything had fallen apart. I still couldn't quite figure out what he intended to do once he got back to the neighbor's house. Was he going to live next door and expect us to not notice? If the first step was to run away and the second was to be picked up by his friends, what was the third step going to be?

To no surprise, Thomas started fighting with some of the other boys, and he ended up punching one of the school administrators in the jaw when they tried to make him go to class. He was charged with assault again, and off to court we went. I was hoping that he would get some sort of consequence greater than the diversion program he was placed in the last time. That program only required him to write letters of apology, which none of us ever received. His public defender told him that he needed to come up with a plan to demonstrate to the court that he was going to change his ways.

Thomas had been speaking with his houseparents about his future. They kept telling us how sweet he was and how much he really wanted to change. Thomas had been helping in the kitchen at the group home. They said he was thinking about going to culinary school and becoming a chef, which they greatly encouraged. He has always enjoyed cooking, just like his father. I didn't know if I believed the wanting-to-change part—maybe in theory and only if he didn't have to work hard for it. I could see him working at a fast-food restaurant one day, but the only way I could envision him getting into culinary school was if he joined Job Corp.

Job Corp is a free government program from the Department of Labor for young people between the ages of sixteen to twenty-four. Thomas just turned sixteen. Job Corp offers on-the-job training in a wide variety of fields, including culinary. If you don't have a high school diploma, they will help you get it by rotating your education week by week. One week focused on high school education and the next on your field of choice. They house you, feed you, provide everything you need for work, and pay you a small wage every week for your labor. They will even relocate you to the best training facility in the country according to what specialty you want to learn. Young people can get a solid education, the government gets skilled laborers, and there are fewer struggling or impoverished people in society—win-win.

The public defender thought it was a great idea. She said she wished she had gotten a free education now that she was stooped in student loan debt. She tried her best to convince him that it would be a great option for him. She said she needed to be able to present the prosecutor with an alternative plan for his future other than jail. He told me, his public defender, and his houseparents that he was willing to go to Job Corp. Before his next court date, I arranged for him to attend an orientation where he could learn more about the program.

When we arrived, the placement coordinator was very clear on the rules and expectations of Job Corp. You couldn't leave campus without permission. There was to be no drugs and no drinking. If you are caught doing so, you would be immediately expelled from the program. They do regular and random drug testing, so he said that if you use even once, you will get caught. If there is any physical fighting, you will be immediately expelled; and if you do not commit to the program, he said you might as well not begin it in the first place.

He made it clear that it wasn't your moma or your grand-momma that was going to get them into the program or keep them in the program. It was completely voluntary, and no one could force them to go. He emphasized that they didn't want to waste their time on people who weren't really looking to change their futures. He then went on to share some amazing testimonies of others who had graduated the program and had been placed in very lucrative positions within their field of training. It seems to be a great opportunity for those who struggle in school or may not have the resources to get training on their own.

After Thomas heard that we couldn't make him go and that he would have to behave and follow the rules and not fight or use drugs, he had set his mind to not go. No matter how much everyone around him wanted him to, he absolutely refused. When his court date arrived, I didn't know what punishment the prosecutor would suggest. The court would be taking into account the culmination of all of his assault charges. His defense attorney wanted to present the judge with an alternative plan for his future, but he didn't have one.

While we were waiting his turn, we watched teen after teen go before the judge for a variety of assault and battery charges against their parents and grandparents. One young boy came out in an orange jumpsuit and shackles. He was charged with robbing a convenience store at gunpoint. Thankfully, Thomas hadn't resorted to guns. I sat there wondering how far he would go if he continued down this path of violence.

Thomas received another smack on the wrist and was placed in the same diversion program as before. He didn't complete the basic requirements the first time around, yet he had been released as having fulfilled his obligation to the court. So here we are, repeating the same useless process again with the same lack of oversight and follow-through. I'm not sure what I was wanting. I guess just something other than "don't do it again" would have been nice.

The stern disciplinary approach from his attorney must have been all for show. I think she was trying to scare him straight, but Thomas doesn't get intimidated easily anymore. This time was about his sixth trip to the courthouse. He had learned he had no reason to fear. Court gave him street cred. He walked the halls like he was a celebrity, saying hello to the other boys he had met in detention or from one of his treatment centers who were also there waiting for their arraignments. He greeted them by name and shook their hands. He was in the land of his people.

*****

We never attended one family session during Thomas's time at this new group home. We were told again and again that Thomas didn't want to see us by his therapist. Christopher went down to take him to lunch one day, and that was when Thomas asked why we hadn't been coming to see him. When his father told him that the therapist had been telling us that he was refusing all this time, Thomas was furious. He started ranting about how much he hated her. Apparently, Thomas had been asking to see us for some time.

We had been hearing conflicting things for a while. The house-parents couldn't say enough nice things about Thomas while the therapist couldn't say any nice things at all. Since this treatment center was outside of our county, our case manager was not authorized to go see him anymore. If he had, maybe this situation would have revealed itself much sooner. Whenever Christopher had called to speak with the director, she always referred him back to the therapist, but the therapist avoided his calls more than she answered them. She clearly didn't like my husband. The feeling was mutual all the way around.

When Christopher took Thomas back to the group home that day, he spoke to the houseparents about the situation, and they confirmed that the therapist had been deceiving us. They said that Thomas had indeed been asking for us. Apparently, they didn't like the therapist either. They said she had been trying to pit all the boys against one another to make them "snitch." The boys that refused to tell on someone else, she was finding ways to punish them. Thomas is many things, but he is not a snitch. He would never tell on a friend. It seems she had been punishing him for his silence since he had gotten there.

We really didn't know what was going on as far as his actual treatment plan. We were never able to arrange a face-to-face meeting, and now we didn't trust anything that the therapist had been telling us over the phone. Christopher complained and demanded that Thomas be assigned to another therapist, but he was told that there wasn't another therapist available. We were about six months into the program, and although Thomas was being cared for well under the supervision of the houseparents, we didn't believe he was benefiting in any way therapeutically.

Thomas ended up running away again. This time, he was careful about what he said on Messenger. The houseparents knew how we were able to follow along with his conversations the last time he ran away. We had asked them not to tell Thomas, but they must have because this time he knew we were somehow able to monitor him. We rarely checked the phone, but when we were told he ran away again, we charged it up to see if we could find out where he was. Looking through his messages, we could tell that he was being careful to not reveal anything too specific. He had gone through and deleted certain things that had been said in his conversation threads.

I kept waiting for him to just reset his password. If he did that, then we would no longer be able to follow along. Instead, he started sending voice texts and deleting whatever he didn't want us to hear. This time we were only able to confirm that his friend was coming to pick him up and that he wanted Thomas to get to a certain area of town so that they could find each other. The area they told him to get to was many miles from the group home. I knew Thomas would have no idea how to get there on foot.

We waited to hear something for hours. We knew the police were out looking for him. I kept an eye out for any activity at the neighbor's house, but the house was quiet. I guess the rendezvous never happened. I wondered how frustrating it must have been trying to communicate and find each other without cell service. His friend had been sending him messages, asking where he was, and Thomas wasn't answering him. He must not have been able to connect to WIFI. His phone had probably died a few hours into his escape.

It wasn't until two days later that the police spotted him walking on the side of the highway in the direction of home. He was picked up and taken back to the group home. About a week later, Christopher received a phone call from the director that Thomas was being released in one week's time. No warning, no discussion. This was six to twelve months before his time there was to be completed. We immediately informed his case manager.

We were in no place to have Thomas back at home. Michal was just beginning to gain some stability, and although my husband and I had a few pleasant moments with Thomas since he had been there, he was still skipping, running away, and assaulting people. Nothing had really changed other than the alleviation of our day-to-day interactions and the stress of him being in the home with us.

Our case manager quickly arranged for an emergency meeting with the SIPP team. They were the ones who had placed Thomas in the treatment facility, and every intake and discharge went directly through them. We assumed they knew of the center's plans to discharge Thomas, but when we told them that we were down to him being discharged in just four days, they were shocked. Before we began to discuss what we were going to do, the head of the team was dialing the phone.

She put the call on speaker and asked the director of the facility why they had not been notified of Thomas's impending discharge. The director claimed they had sent something in writing, but no one on the SIPP team had received anything. The director was reminded that they were legally required to provide a thirty days' written notice before releasing a child. Even if they had just sent something in, they were still violating the thirty days' notice. We sat there quietly while the two of them went round and round.

The others at the table called their people to confirm that nothing had been filed. The insurance company confirmed that they had heard nothing. The nonprofit funding agency that covered whatever the insurance companies didn't confirmed that nothing had been received there either. Once all the confirmations came in, the head of the SIPP team demanded that the director follow proper procedure. She said that they would have to keep Thomas for at least another thirty days and handle his discharge correctly. Then the director asked if she could put the call on hold.

You could have cut the tension with a knife. Everyone in the room seemed flustered. While we waited, the team discussed what options we had. They asked us if we had any idea this was coming, and we assured them that we did not. When the director came back on the line, she said that they fully intended to release him anyway. The person on the SIPP team representing the funding source quickly threatened to pull the funding on all of the youth that they were currently housing. It was only after their funding was directly threatened that the director reluctantly agreed to comply. Before she hung up, she made it very clear that Thomas would be discharged in exactly thirty days from that date.

After that was settled, we began the discussion of what comes next. Within minutes, it was clear that we had exhausted all the resources that were available to us. Finding a third placement was near impossible and would of course take time, much longer than thirty days. Obviously, placing him in a treatment center wasn't working because this was the second one that was discharging him for the very reasons we admitted him in the first place.

Both placements had known he was a flight risk. Both placements had known of his violent tendencies and defiance of authority. It wasn't like they accepted him into their programs unaware of his issues. When Thomas was told by his houseparents that he would be leaving the program, he promised them that he would run away if they sent him home to live with us. He had no intention of returning to our care. He didn't want to stay there, but he didn't want to live with us either.

The head of the SIPP team reviewed his chart, looked over his school records, and discussed his arrests and assault charges with his case manager. They went over his behaviors at school and with the family. When they concluded their review, the leader sat back and asked us if we wanted him back in the home again. Without his behavior changing, we assured her that we did not, but what other choice did we have? That is when she told us that we could refuse to pick him up in thirty days.

She said that they would probably charge us with abandonment, but if we ended up having to go to court, she assured us that she would testify on our behalf. The last thing I wanted was to be thrown into a legal battle. I was tired of having to fight for everything all the time. I knew that refusing to pick him up would get very ugly. We've already had plenty of experience bucking the mental health system. Abandoning him would escalate everything to a whole different level, and doing so had never crossed our minds.

Before he spoke up, I already knew Christopher wouldn't even think of it. When he said as much, she looked at him and said that our adoption should have been labeled as a failed adoption years ago. She went on to say that he has never bonded with us, and he clearly didn't want to be with us. She acknowledged that we had been running around for years now trying to get him the support and help that he needs, but he has only caused us problem after problem, and nothing had changed. He wasn't willing to change.

Failed adoption. I hadn't thought about it that way before. We knew he has never bonded with the family, and he has always wanted to escape and get away from us. I just never thought about labeling it in that way before. We did successfully adopt Thomas, so our adoption didn't actually fail. What she was suggesting would be more accurately termed a *dissolution*. That is where the relationship between an adoptive child and their adoptive parents are legally severed. Some studies report that dissolved adoptions are between 1–5 percent, but these numbers can only reflect children who have reentered the foster care system.

After an adoption is finalized, the child's case is often closed, names are usually changed, and birth certificates and social security cards are reissued under their new identity. Unless they are legally returned to the state, or postadoption services are notified by the adoptive family that there are complications or a runaway situation, accurate tracking in adoption cases is near impossible and believed to be inaccurate.

Although the data is limited and usually very dated due to the difficulty in gathering this type of information, it seems that it is not unheard of for adopted children to end up living with someone else connected with the adoptive family when they are older—if they don't run away and disappear altogether. Families who continue through the whole adoption process do not usually sever their adoption ties when things get difficult but instead choose to remain connected to their adopted child in whatever capacity they can.

What good would it do us to pursue a legal separation with Thomas? He was sixteen years old. Where would he go? Who would take care of him? I guess he would go back into foster care. Then we would have to go to court for how long—weeks, months? I had no idea. What I did know was that I didn't want to have to rehash our struggles with him to a judge. Thomas would be so wounded by our rejection and wouldn't be able to see our side of things. I didn't want to have to defend ourselves and for it to become us against him. Regardless, we were all that he had. One day he may come to his senses and want a family.

I wanted to be done with the struggle, but abandoning him didn't sit right with me. Christopher didn't feel right about it either. He wanted the separation to be on Thomas's terms and not on ours. Whatever the future holds, he wanted us to remain blameless. So, abandoning him was off the table almost as quickly as it was offered as a potential solution. Neither of us were happy at the thought of bringing him home again, but we knew that we had no other viable option. Thomas was coming home in four short weeks. We had to prepare for his homecoming. Michal was going to be devastated.

CHAPTER 19

But from everlasting to everlasting the Lord's love
is with those who fear him, and his righteousness
with their children's children.

—Psalm 13:17

I know that I love Thomas, but sometimes it is difficult for me to feel like I do. My love for him gets buried under all of my emotions and our constant struggles. I love who he really is deep down underneath the brokenness, when I get a glimpse of his true self. The part of him that God created. I have seen him. It has been rare. He has slipped out every now and then for the briefest of moments, but only when he thinks I am not around and he feels he can truly put his guard down. I lament that he feels that he has to guard himself from me. I want him to know freedom and joy—real joy, the joy that only God can bring.

Through this whole process, I have come to realize how conditional my love can be. It is easy for me to love someone who loves me in return. It is easy for me to show love to the people around me who demonstrate kindness and consideration toward me. I read the scriptures about blessing those who curse you, praying for your enemies, offering them your shirt when they have already stolen your coat, and giving them your left cheek when they have already struck you on the right. I understand what God is saying. It seems simple enough to follow these principles until you actually have to follow these principles.

Who can say truthfully that they want to pray blessings over an enemy and sit there while they hurt you without defending yourself in any way? Not me. Honestly, I have gotten upset with people who have borrowed things from me as insignificant as a book and then didn't give it back. I have had to talk myself through my attachment and convince myself that they are just things that don't really matter. After all, they can easily be replaced.

If a thing as insignificant as a book can make me upset with someone, how much more is it to forgive and love someone who outright slanders me, fights me, hurts me, and rejects me? In those times, I believe it is only the love of God that can get me through and can help me keep the correct perspective. I can only truly love because He loves and is love. My human nature says to hurt them back. To make them feel the way they have made me feel.

Love isn't an emotion. Love isn't determined by how I feel. True love is a choice. Feelings come and go. I cannot measure how much I love Thomas by how I feel on any given day. My emotions toward him have been mostly confusion, frustration, rejection, pain, anger, grief, sorrow, and so on. There aren't a lot of happy emotions to draw from in our relationship, but I chose to love him before I even knew him. What he has or hasn't done to me can't change that. I can lose sight of it, but my love still remains. Sometimes I've had to remind myself of that. He can only hurt me because I love him. Otherwise, the things he has done wouldn't affect me so or have any real bearing in my life.

I imagine that my love toward Thomas is a very small representation of God's love toward me. He sent His Son to earth to suffer and die for people who rejected and despised Him. How do you do that? Sometimes it has been a struggle to be gracious and kind with my words when I've been upset with Thomas. That's not even comparable. I am humbled by the way God loves. I cannot wrap my brain around it. I cannot even fathom it. Paul wrote in Ephesians 3:17–19,

> And I pray that you, being rooted and established in love, may have power, together with all the Lord's holy people, to grasp how wide and long and high and deep is the love of Christ, and to know this love that surpasses knowledge, that

you may be filled to the measure of all the fullness of God.

*****

After some last-minute challenges, Thomas was back at home with the family by the end of June. The quiet peace we had enjoyed over the previous seven months was immediately displaced by the inner chaos that he carries. It never fails to amaze me how much one person's presence can alter the atmosphere of a room. Each of us had to naturally shift to accommodate his return, but this time was different. We tried to maintain the status quo as much as possible. He needed to adjust to us this time. We had been fighting hard to pull ourselves out of the pit of trauma, and none of us wanted to fall back into it. We weren't pleased to have him home again, but whether we liked it or not, he was family, and we were his home.

He seemed pleased to be home, but I know that didn't have anything to do with any of us. He was happy to be reunited with his friend. He wasn't speaking to me other than to ask if he could go outside, which meant going to his friend's house. It was strange because sometimes he walked right out the front door, and other times he paused to ask my permission. I couldn't figure out what made him ask one day and what made him not ask the next.

I was letting him pretty much do whatever he wanted. It was summertime, and there was no set routine to dictate his time. Nothing I could do or say to him would change anything he was doing anyway. He was happier out of the house, and his overall contentment was a great benefit to the rest of us. We deliberately chose not to rock the boat.

This time, we knew Thomas was home for good. We had done everything in our power to help him and keep ourselves safe in the process, but we had exhausted our resources. I don't know about anyone else, but I felt trapped knowing we had a year and a half ahead of us until he turned eighteen. I prayed it would be as peaceful and as uneventful as possible. He had always said that he would be gone as soon as he was old enough to leave, so we didn't expect him to stick around after his eighteenth birthday.

Over the years, he has expressed interest in finding his "real parents," especially when he was particularly angry with one of us. We had no problems with his birth parents. My brother called and cussed me out a few times when Thomas first came to live with us. He accused me of being a judgmental Christian and said some pretty hurtful and accusatory things, but I shut him down and told him I wouldn't speak to him as long as he was being abusive. Since then, I hadn't heard anything from him. His birth mother has checked in every so often to get an update and to see a current picture of him. She has never caused us any problems.

We had no intention of keeping Thomas from either one of them. We knew he would want to meet them one day. I suspected that it would be healing for him to see where he came from and to reconnect with them, even if it was only through a short visit. We told him that we would help him connect with them when the time came, but we knew the fantasy of who he imagined they would be wouldn't match up with reality. Fantasies rarely do.

We had heard that he and the neighbor boy were discussing going to California together and starting a life for themselves. They were talking about running a food truck or starting their very own restaurant. I don't know if that was a possibility they were actually thinking of doing together or if Thomas was dreaming up the possibility all on his own. Either way, dreaming was a vital part of coming of age.

When Christopher heard about it, he offered to put some money in Thomas's pocket, pay his cell phone service for a year, and purchase his bus ticket to get him out there once he turned eighteen. He added that we would help him come back home again if he ever changed his mind or if things didn't work out. I don't know if Thomas believed him, but we were willing to help as much as he would allow. We knew he wanted to escape and get as far away from us as possible. California was about as far away as he could go with us living on the east coast.

After a few weeks, fall enrollment for high school had begun. If he decided to go, Thomas would be repeating the ninth grade for the third year in a row. In our state, teens can drop out of school at the age of sixteen without any parental involvement or consent. Since Thomas was over sixteen, we couldn't make him go any longer. Not that we were able to make him go anyway. He was already a dropout without actually being an official dropout. This year, we wouldn't be driving him to the school building day after day. No one would be waiting for him on the front steps. Those days were over. This year was completely up to him.

As he was passing through the living room one evening heading toward his bedroom, I stopped him to ask what his intentions were for the upcoming school year. I told him that it was up to him to decide what he was planning on doing that fall. He seemed annoyed that I had stopped him to ask a question. He shrugged his shoulders and said he didn't know what he was going to do. Then I asked him if he was going to get a job or something because I couldn't allow him to lounge around the house all day long or hang out with his friend and smoke weed day after day and do absolutely nothing with his life. I reminded him that he could still choose to join Job Corps if he wanted to pursue a career in the restaurant industry.

He said, "Man, I got plans. I'm grown. I don't have to tell you nothin'!" Which made me respond with, "You're not grown yet, and as your parent, I have every right to ask you what you are planning to do with your life." He rolled his eyes but didn't respond. After a pause, I asked, "Are you going to go to school, or are you going to get a job? You need to make a decision. If you're going to school, I need to enroll you."

Michal, who was sitting in the room with us, was afraid Thomas was going to start swinging on me when he flashed with anger at my insistence that we have a conversation. He became agitated and was clinching his fists at his sides. Before the first question left my lips, I knew there would be a risk of addressing him head-on, but if I remained silent, I knew he would continue his daily routine indefinitely without any thought of his future.

Since coming home, Thomas had been sleeping in most days until around noon, and then out the front door he would go. He wasn't returning until late in the evening, usually after it was pitch-black outside and everyone else was heading off to bed (even though he knew we wanted him home before dark). I could usually see him hanging out on the neighbor's porch, but there were plenty of times I would catch the two of them walking down the street or jumping into other people's cars and driving off. I think the only reason he was coming home at all was because he knew that was what we expected of him. He wasn't going to give us a reason to send him away. He didn't know that we didn't have anywhere else to send him.

I had been serving in the finance division of our mission agency for some time, but I resigned when he returned home so that I could ensure that Michal was never left alone with him. I'm sure his routine of sleeping in and then leaving the house to spend the day with his friend wouldn't have changed much if I was at the office, but having me home provided a security to Michal that she needed. Being home also ensured that Thomas wasn't breaking into our bedrooms or stealing things. Staying home also allowed my husband the freedom to focus on the ministry, knowing I was keeping an eye out at home.

Watching Thomas come and go every day was infuriating. On one hand, I was thankful he was out of the house and occupying his days elsewhere. On the other hand, I didn't appreciate being used like a hotel. The fact that he felt entitled to do whatever he wanted, whenever he wanted, however he wanted infuriated me. I tried to not let it bother me but his blatant disregard of us, combined with watching him waste away his days running around doing who knows, what was getting under my skin. We were all on edge, but we were determined to avoid any kind of confrontation with him. There was a fake, uncomfortable peace over our interactions, but that was much better than the alternative.

Thomas yelled, "What am I supposed to do then? Where am I supposed to go? I'm only a minor!" To which I replied, "I thought you just said you were grown? You can't have it both ways, Thomas." He can't pick and choose according to what serves him best in the moment. Either he is a minor who needs to follow the rules and answer his mother's questions, or he is a grown adult who can live and do whatever he pleases.

I personally could not continue to enable him through my silence any longer. His friend had already dropped out of high school. Thomas pretty much had as well. The difference was that his friend was getting his GED and considering joining the military or getting a job with a family member. Thomas needed to make some sort of plan as well. I told him he didn't need to go anywhere; he just needed to choose a path. But instead of continuing the conversation, he just shook his head and stormed off to his room and slammed his door.

Two days later, he asked his father if he could spend the night with a friend whose name we had never heard him mention before. Michal knew who he was talking about. It was a boy they had known from school. He lived somewhere in our neighborhood, but Thomas couldn't tell us exactly where. He just kept saying, "That way," and pointing in a general direction without giving any additional information. He wouldn't say what street he lived on, but Thomas said he had been over there many times before (news to me). It wasn't unheard of for Thomas to ask to spend the night at the neighbor's house for us to find out later that the two of them left to spend the night someplace else. We had gotten used to never really knowing where Thomas was most of the time.

Christopher told him he could go. Giving him permission wouldn't change anything other than to release him from his obligation of coming home long enough to sleep that night. Thomas called again the next day and asked if he could stay over again—whatever. His father said that he could, but he needed to come home around lunchtime the following day. Lunchtime came and went. Thomas didn't come home. We expected him to come walking through the door that evening like usual, but he never did. After a few days, we assumed he had gotten the courage to run away. He definitely didn't want to have to go to school or get a job. Running away had solved his dilemma.

Thomas hadn't left the house with anything, and he didn't have a phone for us to reach him. We had been refusing to purchase him smartphones for a while now. He had been caught looking at rape videos and pornography too many times. He has always found a way to work around any apps or tracking programs I had installed on them. Instead, we had been giving him simple flip phones to use. Those always disappeared or ended up smashed to pieces on the driveway. Since we were no longer giving him smartphones, he refused to use anything else out of protest. After a week of no contact, I figured he wasn't coming home, so I packed up his bedroom and set his belongings on the porch. He was going to need clothes wherever he was staying.

I messaged his neighbor friend and told him to let Thomas know that his stuff was out on the porch if he wanted to come by the house and pick any of it up. I woke up a few days later, and everything was gone. He must have come in the middle of the night. Later on, his friend told Isaiah that Thomas had asked him for a ski mask so that he could sneak up onto our porch and get his things without us knowing who he was because a ski mask would prevent us from recognizing him. His friend said he had laughed at his ridiculousness and had called him stupid. Thomas's logic always revealed his simplistic and skewed view of reality.

Days turned into weeks. Thomas never came home. We didn't bother to report him to the police or to the National Center for Missing and Exploited Children because we knew it wouldn't come of anything. Running away is not a crime in our state. There is no law against it. Unfortunately, that means there is very little police officers can do to assist with runaways. Therefore, the burden of finding runaway teenagers rests on the family. If he happened to be found and brought back home, he would most likely run away again. We were done trying to force him to do things.

The statistics of runaways is staggering. The National Runaway Safeline estimates that there is between 1.6 to 2.8 million runaways each year in the United States, some as young as ten years old. They say on any given night, there is approximately 1.3 million youth living homeless on the streets, in abandoned buildings, with friends, or even with strangers. Further studies show that one in seven between the ages of ten to eighteen will run away. *One in seven.* The majority of them report that they ran away due to some sort of physical, emotional, or sexual abuse. One out of every two say they have been expelled, suspended, or have chosen to drop out of school. Thirty-two percent have attempted suicide at some point in their lives, and over 50 percent have some sort of mental illness.

I assumed he was living somewhere nearby, possibly with that friend with whom he had arranged to spend the night. I kept an eye out next door, but the house was quite. Neither Thomas nor the neighbor boy seemed to be around. Maybe they were staying someplace else together. Every time we drove in and out of our neighborhood, I would look down the streets for any indication of where he might be staying. I would often change my route and go down streets I wouldn't normally go down just in case I could catch sight of him. I just wanted to know he was safe and able to feed himself somehow, but I was never able to spot him in our community. For all we knew, he wasn't even in our community.

In a way, I was relieved he was gone. I hated living in the daily tension. Christopher and I had started counting down the days to his eighteenth birthday. Sixteen months was a very short amount of time, yet it was an eternity away. I hate admitting that, but that was how we felt. We didn't want him in the house with us, but we didn't want him homeless or struggling either. Wondering where he was occupied our thoughts continually. I knew he wasn't taking his medication and that the bottle I had put with his things had probably been thrown out. Having him unmedicated posed a variety of potential risks to himself and to the others around him. All I could do was pray for him.

About three months later, Thomas stopped by the house and knocked on the front door. He said he had applied for a job, which was encouraging. He asked me for his social security card. Unfortunately, I didn't have it. Everything he owned, I had packed up and left for him on the front porch months ago. I told him where he could go to get a free replacement card, and he thanked me very politely and then walked off. Just like that. Like we were some random people that he had decided to stop by their house to ask them a question. I stood there watching him walk off, wondering when I would see him again.

Shortly after that, one of Isaiah's friends saw him working in a fast-food restaurant not too far from our home. He said Thomas had just been caught trying to steal cash from the register. He was being yelled at by the manager right there in the middle of the lunch rush. When the friend stopped by to tell us about it, we figured that must have been the job that Thomas had mentioned. I'm sure his days there were numbered. Surely, he was going to get himself fired. We stopped by a few times after that to try to catch him working but never could. One day, we asked one of the employees if he was still working there, and we were told that he wasn't.

It was about seven months after Thomas had run away that his friend came into the restaurant where Isaiah and Michal were working. He told Isaiah that he and a bunch of his friends had gotten a place together and that Thomas had been staying with them for a while. He said that everyone had become frustrated that Thomas wasn't contributing to the household expenses. They all sat him down and told him that he needed to get a job and contribute his share. That must have been about the same time he stopped by, asking for his social security card.

He went on to say that Thomas worked one day a week for a while. When the manager offered him additional shifts, Thomas said he couldn't work them because they were asking him to go in before nine in the morning. Thomas wasn't willing to get up before nine. Eventually, he lost his job, and everyone in the house had voted him out. From there, he had no idea where he went. Thomas's friend said he had grown tired of his erratic behavior, and he was no longer speaking to him. His friend was growing up and making a life for himself. Thomas wasn't growing along with him. Their five-year friendship had ended.

Late one night, I received an urgent Facebook message from his eldest half sister. I had never met her before, and I was surprised that she even knew my name and that she was able to find me. She had just received a panicked phone call from their birth mother, who claimed that Thomas had died. Their mother must have given her my name. Thomas's sister had messaged me right away to see if Thomas was okay or not. Their mother had some struggles with mental illness, so she didn't know if she could trust what she had been told.

Her message gave me a moment of panic. It fed into the fear that something might happen to Thomas, and we wouldn't be there to help him or that we might not find out until it was too late to do anything. I had no idea where he was. It took me a moment to calm down and think rationally. I realized that if he would have died, we would have found out long before their birth mother, who was living states away.

Maybe she was referencing his suicide attempt from years before. We had messaged back and forth a few times over the years, but nothing recently. Maybe she was imagining things. I have no idea. I talked with Thomas's sister well into the night, and she was relieved to hear that he was alive but saddened to hear of his struggles and that he had run away. She had hoped to invite him to stay with her for a while and reunite him with his other biological siblings.

Before Thomas had run away, Isaiah had a dream. In the dream, the family was playing at the beach together. He said Thomas walked out toward the water and turned around and looked at us. After looking back in our direction for a few minutes, he turned away and walked out into the waves. He continued to go farther and farther into the water until the waves overtook him, and he disappeared from view. Isaiah woke up believing that Thomas was going to fade away from the family and eventually disappear. That seemed to be what was happening.

We celebrated the holidays and birthdays without any word from Thomas that winter. We hadn't seen or heard from him since the previous year. When he first left, my thoughts were consumed with worry. I wondered where he was and how he was managing to eat. I wondered how he was doing mentally since he had stopped taking his medication so abruptly. He had missed a court date. His case manager had to close his case and move on to other clients. I let the postadoption coordinator from his birth state know that he had run away. I canceled all of his ongoing doctor appointments.

Our thoughts had been consumed with him and his care for years. Now that he was gone, we had to shift our thinking and begin to let go. There was still a part of me that wondered if he would show up on our doorstep if his situation became dire enough. We were still living in the same place. He knew our phone numbers. He could find us on social media. He could come home any time he wanted to, but deep down I knew he never would.

After months and months, our daughter was still struggling with the fear of him showing up unexpectedly. She continued to wrestle with sleep and felt compelled to continually check the doors at night to make sure they were still locked. As life began to settle, I realized how much I had used television and movies to escape reality. I no longer needed to find ways to occupy my thoughts, and my desire to comfort myself with food began to shift. It was like a cloud was slowly parting. It was finally safe to begin to process through everything and start the healing process.

Christopher told me once that he felt guilt whenever he realized that he had gone a whole day without thinking about him. No matter what, he is still a part of all of us. His presence is still with us even though we now have distance and time between us. He comes up in our family conversations every now and again. We have been able to look back at some of the things he has done or said and laugh together, even within our most traumatic memories. Without any pressing reason to bring up his name, he has begun to fade from our daily lives. The people around us no longer have a reason to ask about how he is doing. If they did, we would have nothing to report. He has become our absent and unmentioned child.

Loss of any kind is hard. We all experience loss in small ways and big ways. Say you have a coworker that you have really enjoyed working with that retires or moves on to another position. You will naturally mourn the loss of your time together, especially if your daily routine is affected. Maybe you lost your lunch buddy in the process. When you relocate to a new city or state, you may gain some great new relationships, but there is always the loss of the ones you've left behind.

When you think of a death within a family, there are social protocols that happen. Family and friends are notified. An obituary is written and shared. Services are conducted. Flowers and food are offered in support. The family's community rallies around them to offer comfort, and bittersweet memories are often shared among tears and laughter. There is an expectation from everyone that you will be working through the grieving process for some time.

Open grieving that is embraced and expected in examples such as a death are not necessarily acceptable in other areas of one's life. I once heard a person tell a woman who had just suffered a miscarriage that she could always try again or just adopt. That may be true, but that isn't acknowledging the pain and the loss or the doubt and the shame associated with infertility issues. It doesn't acknowledge the suffering that these mothers (and fathers) can experience year after year on Mother's Day and Father's Day.

In the same way, the grief and loss associated with a child who has run away can only be truly understood by those who have experienced it firsthand. It isn't something you openly speak about. For us, it's not a secret by any means, but it isn't a casual conversation starter. You don't put memorial stickers on your car or post about it on social media as easily as you would if there had been a death with an expected social mourning period. I would never think to post a status announcing the anniversary of our son's attempted suicide or his running away. Sharing many of the situations our family and other families like ours have gone through is rarely spoken about or publicly acknowledged. Although, it is still loss, and a grieving process must take place.

I haven't stopped being Thomas's mom just because he rejected me. I've spent a lifetime caring for him, and that doesn't stop just because I don't see him anymore. There is a grieving process for all the things we are or will be missing out on with him such as birthdays and holidays. We have experienced a death to our expectations. The hopes and dreams we once held have had to be sacrificed. We have had to learn to lay them all down. We have had to mourn the loss of all the usual teenage milestones such as prom, graduation, teaching him how to drive, and all the ways we could be helping him to settle into college or adulthood. We had begun to mourn those things long before he had run away, but the loss is now magnified by his absence, especially during family events and holiday celebrations.

When we find ourselves in new situations where we are asked how many children we have and how old they are, we list their ages and then share about our eldest three and hope that the omission of the fourth is not noticed. When someone asks what grade he is in, we can usually get away with dodging the question and simply saying that he no longer lives with us. Most people do not pry beyond basic curiosity, but there are those that ask additional questions. We do our best to keep our answers brief and as positive as possible, but any response we give immediately makes the conversation awkward. What do you say when someone tells you that their child has run away from home, and they don't know where he is?

There have been those who have noticed that Thomas hasn't been in a family picture with us in quite a few years. He has refused to participate in family activities and photos long before he actually ran away. With him being institutionalized so many times, there were already gaps of him not being present during family outings and special events. As missionaries, we are regularly sharing pictures and updates of what we are doing. Thomas has been suspiciously absent from those updates for years. We have done our best to keep our family struggles close to home, and we have only shared them one-on-one when someone has expressed genuine concern.

*****

I received a Facebook message from a woman I did not know. She said Thomas was living with her, and she wanted to reach out to us and let us know that he was safe. I have no idea how he met her or what story he had told her, but it was clear that she misunderstood the situation. It seemed she was under the impression we had kicked him out of our home. I guess Thomas would see it that way since his choices were to either go to school or get a job, neither of which he wanted to do. Her message was accusatory. Christopher told me not to respond to her. He said we didn't need to justify ourselves to a stranger.

It is a first-degree misdemeanor to offer a runaway any kind of assistance or aid for more than a twenty-four-hour period. That includes personally taking them in or giving them money to stay in a hotel. In our state, you must be eighteen to be legally able to live separate from your parent or guardian without their permission. He was seventeen, and she was technically breaking the law, but she did the right thing by trying to reach out to us.

It was reassuring to know that he was staying with someone and not out on the streets somewhere alone. If Thomas needed us, we were only a phone call away. We hadn't moved. He knew where we were. We chose not to put ourselves in the position of having to combat the lies he has undoubtedly told her about us. She clearly had a poor perception of who we were. It may have been the wrong approach, but we did not respond. Thomas left voluntarily. No one pushed him out. No one threatened him. No one abused him.

Other than that one message, we have heard nothing else for many months. I figured he would show up if he needed something from us. I guess no news is good news. Other than mental illness, he has always been very physically healthy. I assumed someone would contact us if any kind of emergency arose, and three months before Thomas's eighteenth birthday, we received an unexpected phone call from a caseworker. She was vague and combative from the start. Apparently, we had been reported for neglect, and she wanted to schedule an appointment to conduct a home inspection. There was no need to conduct a home inspection. All the people living in our home were over the age of eighteen. My husband absolutely refused.

As I was sitting there listening to their conversation, I could see Christopher was getting more and more frustrated. He kept asking her why she was calling. He wasn't frustrated that she was trying to do her job and follow up with a report. It was the disrespectful way that she was speaking to him. After she accused him of abandonment and he told her that Thomas had not been abandoned, she actually laughed and mocked him. That was when he proceeded to say, "Let's get something perfectly clear." When those words come out of his mouth, I know he had reached the height of his patience.

He very clearly explained our situation and the fact that Thomas ran away voluntarily more than a year prior. He listed off his diagnoses and all the treatment centers he had been in and the fact that he was a part of SIPP. Once he did that, her tune immediately changed. The caseworker acknowledged that she knew Thomas was not living with us. She confirmed that he was living with a friend and his grandmother and that the grandmother was willing to allow him to continue to stay with her. The caseworker went on to say that she did not have a problem with his current living arrangement, which gave further credence to not needing that home inspection.

She said that Thomas has been refusing to speak with her. That was no surprise. We knew he wouldn't be interested in meeting with a caseworker. He didn't want to be sent back home. She couldn't tell us who had reported us, but she said Thomas had gone to the hospital with stomach problems. We were probably reported by a doctor, which they are legally required to do. When the hospital tried to look up his insurance, the caseworker said it had been canceled. We hadn't canceled it. He has insurance until his eighteenth birthday per our adoption agreement. She requested a copy of his insurance cards before ending the call. Other than a potential insurance issue, there wasn't anything further that needed to be discussed because he would be of legal age in three short months.

CHAPTER 20

For the Lord is good; his steadfast love
endures forever, and his faithfulness
to all generations.
—Psalm 100:5

I asked Christopher if he had the choice, knowing what he does now, would he go back to the very beginning and adopt Thomas all over again? He gave an immediate and resounding yes. When I ask myself that same question, I am not so sure. I don't think I would willingly put myself and the rest of the family through it all over again, knowing the struggle and the ill effects it would have on everyone. I don't regret it. I wouldn't be who I am without having gone through it. My children wouldn't be who they are without having gone through it either. We are stronger. We are more unified as a family because of it.

The struggle actually pulled the five of us closer together. Having rallied together against a common foe helped us survive. I hate referencing Thomas as a foe, but in the midst of our most trying times, that is how the rest of us felt. It was us against him—circling of the wagons. That was never our intention, but it had become our reality. Unfortunately, there are countless families out there who don't survive the hardship that a difficult adoption brings. There are plenty of everyday challenges that can make staying connected as a family extremely difficult. When you add any kind of additional trauma, fear, doubt, insecurity, and conflict (to name a few), many families do not survive. I am so thankful that mine did because we have had every reason not to.

If I try to evaluate our experiences through Thomas's perspective, I wonder if he would have been better off being placed in a family without other children. Would some of his struggles been eliminated had he not had siblings? I also wonder if he would have benefited from a more tender and soft-natured mother. Then again, could a mother like that have stood toe-to-toe with him when he was raging and throwing things at them? Could they have held their ground and fought back the way that I have had to? These types of questions I will never know the answer to, and they are all hypothetical anyway. We cannot reverse time. Ultimately, it doesn't matter. For whatever reason, God chose us to step in and be his parents—for better or for worse.

If I did have the chance to start over with Thomas, I know there are things I would do and say differently, of course. I would be much more aggressive and proactive with his care from the very beginning. I would be armed with greater knowledge to fight for the services he needed much sooner than he got them. I would never have settled for therapists who didn't understand RAD and ODD. I would be more insistent with sharing our familiar connection so that maybe he could understand that he isn't living with strangers and that he isn't really that different from the rest of us. In short, I would address his identity issues more aggressively. I would definitely be more aware spiritually and would seek breakthrough in that realm much earlier than I had.

If we would have known what we know now, there might have been a chance to change our outcome. Thomas's future might look completely different than it currently does. Maybe. Maybe not. There is no way to know. I think most parents would have things that they would do or say differently in hindsight. Hindsight really is twenty-twenty. No one is perfect, adult or child. Unfortunately, we cannot reverse time. There are no do-overs. We can only strive to do our best with what we know at the time.

My prayer is that my story finds itself in the hands of those who need to know that they are not alone. Only about 2 percent of the United States population has adopted. Although that is such a small percentage, with a population of over 328 million people, 2 percent still leaves millions of families directly affected by adoption. There are many families like my own that find themselves silenced within their struggle of caring for their adopted children. Like most things, it will take a lot more education and awareness for those not affected by adoption to be able to understand and support the families that do adopt.

Fortunately, adoption is a more commonly addressed topic in articles and media now more than ever before. There are resources out there, but adoptive families have to search them out. When I've come across a good article or blog post from another adoptive parent, they have usually left me in tears because someone else out there gets the struggle. At one time, I thought about joining a support group or online forum, but I chose not to. For a while, every aspect of my life was consumed with Thomas and his care. My thoughts, my conversations, my time was completely centered around him and his needs. He needed that from me, but I couldn't give more than I already was. I needed those breaks where my thoughts could focus on something else. I needed moments of normal.

I've sat in group therapy sessions where all the parents took turns sharing their horrific stories. One child was trying to murder the stepmom, another had tried to set their house on fire, a third had attempted to kill their baby sibling. In the end, we could all listen to one another; but no one, including the therapist, had any advice or additional support to offer other than what all of us were already doing. It did not encourage me to hear their stories, and I felt ill equipped to offer any kind of encouragement in return. I couldn't figure out how to help my own child. I definitely didn't have advice for anyone else's. I suspect none of us were in a place to offer support. I think we were all shell-shocked. On the other side of things, I think I could be an encouragement now, but definitely not then.

I have never heard of these kinds of traumatic stories being spoken of outside of social services and mental health circles. Maybe that is due to the individualized and personal nature of each family's struggle. Hopefully, it is also because these types of cases are rare. I would proudly walk or run to raise awareness for breast cancer. There isn't societal shame in being diagnosed with a disease like that. Those suffering from cancer can openly discuss their illness and their course of treatment if they so choose. When they do, I would say that they are usually met with an outpouring of compassion and support. Mental illness and adoption issues are unfortunately treated very differently.

Openly discussing my son's threats to harm us or our pain from his attempted suicide makes people uncomfortable. They don't know how to respond. It's not that people don't care. There just isn't a social construct in place to help people respond to those types of situations. Suicide, depression, and violence are not usually things you take to the streets to advertise openly. Those of us who are affected by family members with mental illness are many, but it isn't something that comes up in everyday conversation. When it does, we are often misunderstood and unfairly judged, especially as a parent of a child who is mentally ill. Maybe it is the extreme circumstances we have dealt with that so many other parents cannot begin to even fathom.

I was attending a youth conference once, and a teenage girl about the same age as Thomas at the time came on stage to share her story. She shared about how she had been adopted into a loving family. She said she had struggled, and things hadn't always been easy for her, but she ended her brief story with how thankful she was to have been adopted. Afterward, she and her adopted family hugged. It was sweet and wonderful and crushing. My eyes welled up with tears as everyone around me clapped and cheered. We like happy endings, but not everyone gets them.

I feel betrayed by the smiling faces on the front of adoption brochures. Don't get me wrong, I think adoption is beautiful. Children need loving, well-intentioned families to rescue them and care for them. Adoption is the heart of the Father. I just wish there was a balance, a reality, an understanding associated with adoption that says it is okay when things don't turn out as perfectly as you had hoped. Adoption is a lot of work, and it is not for the faint of heart. My hope is that everyone who adopts, especially from foster care, goes into it with eyes wide open and counting the cost. I think having an unrealistic fantasy of a perfect family only makes everything that much harder. There are no perfect families, adopted or otherwise.

*****

Thomas reached eighteen and is officially an adult—as adult as anyone is at that young age. Although we have reached a major milestone in our relationship with him and he is now free in all aspects to live his life without our interference or input, we will forever be his parents. Whether or not he wants to acknowledge us in his life will never change who we are to him. I will always be his mother, and my husband will always be his father. We will be there for him in whatever capacity he allows us to be. We will always love him. We will always think of him and wonder where he is and how he is doing. Maybe one day we will see him again.

The story of the prodigal son in Luke 15 has taken on a deeper meaning for me since Thomas ran away. I now have a prodigal son of my own out in the world somewhere doing who knows what. I know the parable has many layers of meaning. One of which is a representation of this world and the heart of Father God to have humanity return to Him as sons with full rights of inheritance. It also shows the heart of an earthy father longing for the return of his rebellious son.

I have wondered if I would be so gracious as to open my arms to Thomas as freely as the father in the parable had done. The father was running toward his son while he was still a long way off. He started running before any repentance was given. He started running before any explanation or acknowledgment of wrongdoing left his son's lips. The father was just running to embrace him and welcome him home unconditionally. The reality of that has made me evaluate my willingness to forgive so freely. Could I open my heart so willingly toward Thomas? I can only pray that I have the opportunity to find out. I know my husband would take off running without a second thought.

Just like the son in the parable, Thomas has been given an amazing inheritance. When we adopted him, he was afforded all the same spiritual blessings and rights that were made available to our other three children. Our children are the children of parents who have faithfully followed God, who have sacrificially laid down their lives in service to His kingdom. We don't have an abundance of wealth to offer them, but what we have to offer them is abundant in the sight of God. I can say that confidently because I know the abundant love and favor that we walk in. Our lives have been far from easy. We have faced tremendous challenges in every aspect of life, but we rest confidently in the shadow of the Almighty.

One of the biggest lessons my husband and I have learned through this process is just how good God is. He knew what He was asking of us from the beginning. He knew what we would walk through when we chose to obey Him and set things in motion to adopt Thomas. He wasn't surprised at the outcome. We may have been, but God knew all along. He didn't ask us to take Thomas in to cause us pain and heartache. I believe the whole plan was a rescue mission, and that rescue mission continues to this day. He has promised me that He will be relentless in His pursuit of Thomas. He has promised that He will speak to him in his dreams.

I think and pray for Thomas often, but I rest in knowing that God is at work. There is nothing more me or my husband can do. We have had to completely release him to the care and protection of God. Letting go has been a slow and difficult process. It has challenged our belief and faith in God. We have had to come to a place where our trust in Him outweighs our fears. Jeremiah 29:11 says God's intention is to prosper Thomas and not to harm him. He wants to give a hope and a future to him. I know He wants to do the same for me and for the rest of my family. I have had to reconcile that truth against how things appear in the natural.

God goes on to say in verse 12–14, "Then you will call on me and come and pray to me, and I will listen to you. You will seek me and find me when you seek me with all your heart. I will be found by you," declares the Lord, "and will bring you back from captivity." His heart toward Thomas is so good. If Thomas seeks Him, he will find Him. When he finds Him, his captivity will finally end. He will find his healing and freedom. I know that God will be with him, pursuing him, and waiting for him every single day of his life. My prayer now is that Thomas would open his heart to Him.

Because I trust God, because I have grown to understand His character, I can find rest when circumstances are out of my control. I guess that is one thing I have learned over the years because very few things have ever been in my control. We have had to rely on God to work things out for us just as Romans 8:28 says, "And we know that for those who love God all things work together for good, for those who are called according to His purpose." I'm not sure how He will turn all of this to good, but God has been faithful to us all along this journey. Without Him, I believe our situation would have been far worse. Thomas probably would have died the night he hanged himself. There was no reason for his belt to have broken. I believe God has intervened on our behalf numerous times and in ways we may never know.

I can look back over our time with Thomas and say confidently that we willingly obeyed God and did all that He had asked of us. We did everything within our power to help him and to be the best parents we could be to him. I think we went above and beyond what many other parents would have done in our situation. In spite of being told to walk away and abandon him, we remained steadfast and true. We stand blameless in whatever accusations we have faced or will ever face.

I do not know what will become of our relationship. Our roles as his mother and father will never end, even if we never have the opportunity to speak to him again. All we can do now is pray for him and hope that one day there will be a restoration of our relationship. God is a God of restoration. The whole Bible is about restoring mankind to God and repairing that broken relationship. So I have no doubt that God desires to repair our relationship with Thomas. In the meantime, I have to rest in the confidence of a good God who is continually working on my behalf to make that happen. I have to let go and let God handle it from here.

I do not know the future. I wish I did, but my hope is not birthed out of what I can see but rather what I expect to happen in the future. I can have hope because I know who I serve. I can have confidence that God will continue to work on my behalf, on my family's behalf, and most importantly on Thomas's behalf because I trust in Him. I can put my faith in Him. Does that mean that everything will work out in the end? Not necessarily. I pray that it will, but there is this pesky little thing called free will. God will not force surrender and obedience on Thomas. That would be slavery, and God is freedom, not oppression. Even if Thomas has an amazing, supernatural encounter with Him, he would still have to surrender his will to God's. At this point, I know that Thomas is not ready to do that. I can only pray that one day he will be ready because I know God will be there waiting, and so will we.

It has been a healing process for me to write out my family's story. I clearly heard the voice of the Lord tell me to write it down in a book the same night we admitted Thomas into his first long-term treatment center. It has taken some time to get to a place where I could begin to process through all that has happened in our sixteen-year, and counting, adoption journey. Far more has happened than what could ever be recounted in this book. I pray that what needed to be said was said and that God uses it as He sees fit.

One of my favorite scriptures is Revelation 12:11: "They overcame him by the blood of the Lamb and by the word of their testimony." Testimonies are powerful and impacting. They tell of God's goodness and faithfulness. They tell of triumph in spite of struggle and hopelessness. They reveal the heart and character of God and His perfect love toward all of us. Even though my story continues and is not yet complete, there is so much me and my family have walked through that testifies of God's goodness. I don't have to wait for some sort of conclusion to share what He has already done in our lives. He deserves my praise even when circumstances are not what I want them to be.

It is only by God's grace that my family has survived, and not only survived but is starting to thrive. He has protected us relentlessly over the years—physically, emotionally, and spiritually. He has protected Thomas's life repeatedly. There is no way we will ever know all the ways God has worked, and is still working, in and through all of us. He is restoring my heart and the heart of my husband. He is healing my daughter one layer at a time. My sons have worked through their anger toward Thomas and toward God and are now faithfully serving in His kingdom.

I hope that the reading of my story will somehow encourage others who are or have been through a difficult adoption with the truth that they are not alone. For a while, I shut myself off from everything and everyone around me. I focused on what I had to do and didn't do much else. I felt so isolated because there was a huge part of my life where I didn't have anyone else outside of my immediate family to share it with that would believe me and support me. I had no one else to lean on. My husband and I could only lean on each other so much because we were both struggling to stand.

Every time I found myself in the presence of God, I wept. The sorrow I felt was so great. I didn't want to feel it. I didn't want to cry every time the music played at church. I didn't want to feel so vulnerable and emotionally raw for everyone else to see. Feeling His love was hard, so I pulled away and stopped engaging. I kept myself right on the edge. I didn't distance myself, but I didn't enter in fully either. I knew I needed to just jump in and make a mess of myself, but I didn't. I couldn't.

God was there with me the whole time. He saw the way I was trying to protect myself from the full weight of my emotions. He was like the father in the parable, ready to run to me as soon as I showed up. Ready to embrace me. Ready to adorn me with His goodness. He saw me and has waited for me. He sees you in your struggle as well. He knows what you are facing, and He is with you. Rest in Him. Don't hold back like I did. When you feel weak and discouraged, He is strong. He hears your prayers. Trust that He is there for you and working on your behalf.

For those who have not adopted, I hope that my story has been able to increase your awareness and understanding so that you can become a support and a friend to those who have. The most supportive thing you can offer is a listening ear. You don't have to understand everything. You don't even have to believe what they say, but for goodness' sake, don't tell them that you are struggling to believe them. If you do, they will undoubtedly become hurt and will probably never open up to you again. If you are truly their friend and you know them and their character, then trust in what they have to say. Why would they lie to you?

You don't have to have something wise to say to them. I think the best thing that you could say is, "That really sucks." We aren't looking for you to fix anything. You can't. We just need you to cry with us. Hug us. Let us know that you are there for us in any capacity we need. For me, being able to get out of the house and have a "normal" evening with a friend is more valuable than gold. Find out what your friend or family member needs and be that for them.

Those that are considering adoption, do it. Even after experiencing all that we have gone through, I believe adoption is beautiful. There is a child out there who needs you, but I would caution you to adopt with eyes wide open. My story will not be like your story. Do your research. Take classes. Educate yourself. Rally supporters around you that will walk the journey with you in the good times and in the difficult times. Become your child's greatest advocate. No one else will care for them the same way that you will. Speak up. Fight for them, and most importantly, stay strong and after having done all, *stand*.

ABOUT THE AUTHOR

Sheila never considered herself a writer but as a pastor, worship leader, teacher, and missionary leader. She has used her writing abilities countless times to develop her own children's ministry curriculum, leadership training manuals, Bible study materials, and missionary resources. She has even written a family cookbook for her four children. Needless to say, writing has infused itself into every aspect of her life. On most days, you'll find her typing away on her computer, sharing the latest missions story, updating website content, or working on a new design project. When she's not writing, you will find her enjoying a movie with her husband, singing at the top of her lungs with her daughter, or learning the latest worship song on her piano.

CPSIA information can be obtained
at www.ICGtesting.com
Printed in the USA
BVHW071311141019
561050BV00002B/156/P